D0806677

John Seely

Oxford Secondary English

Understanding

A GCSE Course

Oxford University Press

Oxford University Press, Walton Street, Oxford OX2 6DP

Oxford New York Toronto
Delhi Bombay Calcutta Madras Karachi
Petaling Jaya Singapore Hong Kong Tokyo
Nairobi Dar es Salaam Cape Town
Melbourne Auckland

and associated companies in
Beirut Berlin Ibadan Nicosia

Oxford is a trade mark of Oxford University Press

© Oxford University Press 1986
First published 1986
Reprinted 1987 (twice)

ISBN 0 19 831152 4

Typesetting by MS Filmsetting Limited, Frome, Somerset
Printed in Great Britain by The Bath Press, Bath

Contents

Introduction

This book is designed to prepare students for the *Reading* component of the GCSE English examination.

The National Criteria state that syllabuses should include the assessment of reading as a central part of work in English, and that:

1 Material used should be both 'literary and non-literary';
2 There should be 'a variety of kinds of written response from the closely structured to the open-ended';
3 These can usefully include 'structured sets of short-answer questions which follow the sequential patterns of the text';
4 Written response to close reading 'should extend where appropriate, to more than a paragraph'.

The interpretation of these criteria by different examination boards shows considerable variation, but all boards require the use and assessment of both intensive and extensive reading, either through a formal test, or by means of coursework, or both. Practice in extensive reading is beyond the scope of this book. Instead, **Understanding** has been produced to give guidance and practice in intensive reading. It sets out to develop good attitudes towards reading and effective reading strategies and techniques. It then provides practice in these.

The book is in three sections:

Section A: approaches to reading. This is a short section which introduces a number of approaches to texts and gives practice in useful strategies and techniques. The section is progressive in structure and is designed for use at the beginning of a GCSE course.

Section B: non-literary material. These units may consist of a single text, with illustration, but more often they are 'packages' of different kinds of material (text, data, tables, graphs, diagrams etc.) linked by their subject matter. Written material used is intended to inform or persuade, or a mixture of the two. The response demanded includes both questions and extended writing assignments. These often require writing in a 'closed' situation, as described in the National Criteria.

Section C: literary material. Some of the texts used are extracts but seven are complete short stories. Again the units contain both short-answer questions and more extended responses, including directed writing.

In Sections B and C the units are arranged according to reading difficulty and complexity. Each has three stages:

Introductory units
These guide the student to practise the techniques introduced in Section A and refer the reader to the relevant pages of that section.

Transitional units
These still give some guidance, but the reading and writing make heavier demands upon the user.

Test units
Units which give no guidance to the student, but which require him or her to use the skills which have been developed. These are suitable for either practice or testing.

Section A: Methods

1. Looking at reading

2. Sorting out the facts

3. Reading between the lines

1. *Looking at reading*

Reading is a skill that we take for granted. Yet there are people who either find reading very difficult or cannot read at all. To them a city street may look like this:

Try to work out the meanings of the signs you can see in the picture:
1 How many can you work out?
2 What kind of thing do they say?
3 How do you know?

Kinds of reading

Before we can really understand anything we read we need to work out a number of things about it:
- The kind of reading material it is
- What its purpose is
- What kind of person wrote it
- What kind of person it was written for

Read the extracts that follow and for each one answer the list of questions at the end.

A

MISCELLANEOUS FOR SALE

NOTARRIANI ice cream machine complete with matching 7.5 kva alternator. £450 o.n.o. Tel. 031–249–0501.

B The canary

The song of canaries
Never varies
And when they're moulting
They're pretty revolting.

Ogden Nash

C

ENGLISH

PAPER 2

Tuesday 31st April 1999   2.00pm–3.45pm

You are allowed 15 minutes reading time before the examination begins.
During this period you may read the paper, but you must not write anything.

D

E

ARALDITE *Rapid*

IF ARALDITE GETS ONTO CLOTHING

It is essential to remove it before it sets. Scrape off as much as possible and wipe with clean cloth soaked with white spirit. White spirit can also remove liquid adhesive from metals and other materials. But be careful. White spirit is inflammable and can irritate the skin.

F

Ist XI

The following have been selected to represent the school against St Martin's, Burnham, on Saturday 14th March. Kick-off 10.15 a.m.

A Harper

J Bowes

Questions

1 How would you describe each type of reading material?
2 What is its purpose?
3 What kind of person wrote it?
4 What kind of person was it written for?

Types of text: fact

A very simple way of classifying texts is into **fact** and **fiction**. Many examination boards use this classification and ask candidates to answer questions on two passages: one factual, the other fiction.

Factual writing can have a number of purposes, one of the commonest is **to inform**, to tell the reader something. Factual texts that are intended to inform can be divided into three main groups:

Description

Descriptive writing tells you what something looks like or is like.

Small and frail-looking, with white hair cut in the Roman style, and a fanatic's eyes gleaming from deep-set sockets, he is now in his sixties. In his youth he was deeply religious, and spent two years training for the Roman Catholic priesthood.

Exposition

Exposition is writing that explains things – how and why things are as they are.

Skin usually falls into specific age cycles. Between 15 and 25 years, apart from the odd spot or blackhead, the skin has a youthful bloom. At this age it can take a beating (and often does with too much sun, alcohol, junk foods, late nights) and still survive. This is simply because the cell renewal rate is rapid, occurring every 19 to 20 days.

Reporting

A report tells the reader what happened on a particular occasion. It usually sets out the events in the order in which they happened, but it may change the order if it makes things clearer or more interesting.

Holidaymaker Stan Heeney, 35, from Spalding, had a miraculous escape yesterday. Stan was walking on the moors near Pengower in Cornwall when suddenly the ground opened up and he fell fifty feet into a disused tin mine.
'I thought I'd had it' confessed Stan, recovering in Truro Hospital last night, 'but fortunately there were some other people on the moors. I shouted for help and after a while two people heard my cries and managed to find where I was.'

Another very common purpose for factual writing is **to get the reader to do something**. The writer may wish to instruct the reader in how something should be done, or to provide a set of rules which should or must be obeyed. On the other hand the intention may be **to persuade** the reader to agree with a particular point of view.

This kind of writing can be divided into three common types:

Rules and instructions

Assuming that you are right-handed, you should be holding the rod with the right hand grasping the butt of the rod either above, or just forward of, the reel, with your index finger crooked about the line and the bale-arm of the reel open. Your forearm should rest along the remainder of the butt, and the rod can either be held fully out to your right, parallel to the water, or across your body pointing to the left.

Statements of belief

When it comes to sports I am not particularly interested. Generally speaking, I look upon them as dangerous and tiring activities performed by people with whom I share nothing except the right to trial by jury. It is not that I am totally indifferent to the joys of athletic effort – it is simply that my idea of what constitutes sport does not coincide with popularly held notions of the subject.

Expressing an argument

Surely Mr Morgan, the retired ambulanceman who is reported to be campaigning to ban the kids from Westfaling Street BMX track, must realize the dangers of putting these riders back on the footpaths and streets of our city? He is reported as saying he wants the park for the children to play in. Isn't this exactly what the BMX track encourages?

Types of text: fiction

There are four main types of writing the reader expects to find in a novel: narrative, description, dialogue, thoughts.

Narrative

Narrative writing 'tells the story':

He tightened his belt and began to climb. All those big rocks were loose and very smooth. He had to jump from one to another, gripping for footholds with his hands and toes, crouching like a dancer and then jumping, curled up in a ball, so that he landed on all fours. He got almost to the end of the pass when he missed his foothold. He swayed for a moment out over the sea. Then he gasped and swung himself in towards the cliff, grasping a pointed rock that projected. The rock held his weight until he reached another foothold in the entrance to the fissure. Then as he strained at it further to raise himself and thrust himself forward, it gave way with a rumbling noise. Terrified at finding the rock coming loose with his hands, he hurled himself forward on his face and clung to the wet floor of the fissure. He lay still.

Narrative writing is concerned with questions like: What happened first? In what order did things happen? Why did this event happen? What effects did it have?

Description

Descriptive writing tells us what people, places and things are like:

a)   He appeared less than his medium height for he was heavily built with very broad shoulders. Immensely powerful in his youth, he had run to seed in his old age and now his belly sagged in folds and he waddled as he walked. Above a short thick neck, his face was veined and covered with silver bristles; his eyes, small and red-rimmed, were hot and arrogant.

b)   That evening ... I stood watching the sun go down behind reedbeds that stretched to the world's end. High overhead, banks of cirrus cloud, blown to tattered streams, ranged from ebony to flaming gold and the colour of old ivory, against a background of vermilion and orange, violet, mauve and palest green. From all around, as if the Marshes breathed, came the massed voices of frogs, an all-pervading pulse of sound, so sustained that the mind ceased to take note of it. More than any other, even than the crying of geese in winter, this was the sound of the Marshes.

Descriptive writing is concerned with questions like: Where does the story take place? What does the character look like? What is his or her personality? What does a particular scene look, sound, feel like?

Dialogue

Most novels use dialogue between characters:

'You'll shoot?'

'Of course I'll shoot.'

'I've got an idea,' Anne said. 'We don't want to take any risks. Give me your overcoat and hat. I'll put them on and slip out first and give them a run for their money. In this fog they'll never notice till they've caught me. Directly you hear the whistles blow count five slowly and make a bolt. I'll run to the right. You run to the left.'

'You've got nerve,' Raven said. He shook his head. 'No. They might shoot.'

'You said yourself they wouldn't shoot first.'

'That's right. But you'll get a couple of years for this.'

'Oh,' Anne said, 'I'll tell them a tale. I'll say you forced me.' She said with a trace of bitterness, 'This'll give me a lift out of the chorus. I'll have a speaking part.'

Raven said shyly, 'If you made out you were my girl, they wouldn't pin it on you. I'll say that for them. They'd give a man's girl a break.'

Dialogue can be used to: tell us about characters; tell us about relationships; give us additional information about scenes the writer has not described; add to the impact of a particular scene.

Thoughts

Sometimes the writer tells the reader what one of the characters is thinking:

One day a big locust whirred dryly past her head, and she jumped up with a cry, scattering her sewing things. He laughed at her as she bent about picking them up, shuddering. She went into the house to fetch the tea, and he began to read. But presently he put down the book and, yawning, noticed a reel of pink cotton that she had missed, lying in a rose bed.

He smiled, remembering her. And then he became conscious of a curious old mannish little face, fixed upon him in a kind of hypnotic dread. There, absolutely stilled with fear beneath his glance, crouched a very big locust. What an amusing face the thing had! A lugubrious long face, that somehow suggested a bald head, and such a glum mouth. It looked like some little person out of a Disney cartoon. It moved slightly, still looking up fearfully at him. Strange body, encased in a sort of old-fashioned creaky armour. He had never realized before what ridiculous-looking insects locusts were! Well, naturally not; they occur to one collectively, as a pest – one doesn't go around looking at their faces.

Describing a character's thoughts is a useful way of helping the reader to understand more clearly: that character; his or her relationships with others; the meaning of a situation.

THE READING ROUTE

1. What is it?

What kind of text am I reading?

Is it a story? A set of instructions?

An argument? An explanation?

Does knowing this help to understand it better?

3. What is the detailed meaning?

What are the problem paragraphs / sentences / words?

Can I work out their meanings from the rest of the text?

Can I think it through?

Can I make an intelligent guess?

2. What is it for?

Who wrote it? For what kind of reader?

What effect did the writer want to have on the reader?

Why am I reading it?

What do I hope to get out of it?

4. What is the pattern?

Can I divide the text up into sections?

How many? What is each section about?

How do the sections link together?

5. Does it say anything between the lines?

Does it take anything for granted? What?

Does it hint or suggest things without stating them?

Does it present opinions as if they were facts?

ONE WAY

STOP

DON'T WALK

SLO

The *reading route* is a way of making sure that you ask yourself the right questions when you are studying a text. It has five stages, as you can see.

All five stages are dealt with in the first part of this book.

Stage 1: pp. 6–11; 26–27.   Stage 2: pp. 6–11; 28–29.   Stage 3: pp. 18–25.
Stage 4: pp. 14–17.   Stage 5: pp. 26–27; 30–37.

Exercise

For each of the short texts that follows, answer as many of the questions on the route as you can.

A

Meals boycott

Students at the Royal National College for the Blind, staged a lunchtime boycott on Tuesday to protest over the quality of their food.

A students' spokesman said they were fed up with an endless supply of sausages and chips and mourned the absence of boiled eggs and porridge for breakfast.

'The cheese on toast is rubbery, the pizza is fried hard and we have tons of beans,' said the spokesman.

College principal, Mr Lance Marshall, said: 'The weather is pretty awful and is probably getting them down a bit.'

B

Route 156   **EDALE-EYAM**   13 miles   20 km

OS 1:250 000 nos 6, 5 or 7
Bartholomew's 1:100 000 no. 29
OS 1:50 000 nos 119, 110
1 inch:1 mile Peak District tourist map
Edale See Route 113. Also links with Routes 114, 115
Rowland Cote Edale YH
Mam Tor, Castleton and **Bradwell** See Route 113
Eyam Moor Fine views and a Bronze Age stone circle (DoE)
Eyam See Route 157

C   **The Blitz begins**

On that Saturday afternoon Goering and Kesselring are said to have stood on the cliffs of Cap Gris Nez and watched the bombers of 2nd Air Fleet form up and set off for London, while the escorting fighters took up their positions above and below the Heinkels and Dorniers. That was at approximately four o'clock. Further to the south, bomber after bomber of Sperrle's 3rd Air Fleet, forming the second wave of the attack, roared along the runways of Normandy and Brittany and was airborne. That afternoon well over 300 bombers, escorted by about 600 fighters, flew against London.

2. *Sorting out the facts*

Seeing the pattern

In order to understand a text properly, you need to be able to work out the pattern it follows. This involves seeing how the different parts of it fit together and relate to each other. With some kinds of text this is quite easy – in a story, for example, events often happen in a simple sequence which is easy to follow. At other times – with complicated arguments or explanations, for example – it is more difficult. The first two exercises in this unit give practice in seeing the pattern in a text.

Exercise One

In the short text that follows, six sentences have been missed out. They are listed in the wrong order at the end. Read the text and work out which sentence should go in which space. Then write down the number of the space and the letter of the sentence which you have chosen to fill it.

'They taught us that no amount of exercise could do you any harm,' said the coach. — 1 — No one dreamed that men over the age of 40, non-athletes, would be running 50, even 100 miles a week on hard surfaces. That is what is happening in the 1980s.'

What could not have been predicted either, 30 years ago, was that six-year-olds would be selected for competitive gymnastics in Britain, and that some would be pushed so hard that the growth of their bones would be impaired.

We live in a new sporting age, far removed from the genteel amateurism of the past, and the risks sportsmen and women now run are many times greater. — 2 — The problem is that the extremes are becoming more and more commonplace.

Take the case of Katy Parkins from Buckinghamshire. Two years ago, at the age of 11, she started serious gymnastics. She looked promising, and her coach encouraged her to do more. Soon she was training so hard that she developed an 'over-use' injury of the spine – osteochondritis. — 3 — But her coach advised her to 'exercise through the pain'.

'She said it would just get better,' said Katy. 'It hurt worst when I was arching my back to do crabs. I was in a lot of pain. Then one day, when I was ice-skating, my back locked completely, and I couldn't move. My friends had to carry me to the side.'

— 4 — According to the sports surgeon John Williams, who eventually diagnosed Katy's problem, it was the kind of advice given more and more often by coaches and parents anxious for success.

Dr Williams is the medical director of the Farnham Park Rehabilitation Centre in Buckinghamshire, one of the few specialists centres for treating sports injuries. — 5 —

'I feel in general,' he said, 'that when a child talks of pain, that's the time to stop. The coach should make sure that there is proper screening of children in their care, to prevent over-use injuries, and specialist help should be sought where any problem is suspected. — 6 — I feel that, more and more often, children are coming under pressure to carry on, when they should be told to stop.'

A The more she exercised, the more it hurt.

B But that was in the 1950s.

C In Katy's case, if she had carried on with her gymnastics, she could well have suffered permanent injury to her back.

D Sport, taken to extremes, can seriously damage your health.

E He sees hundreds of sport-damaged patients each year, and gymnastics is one of his chief worries.

F The coach told Katy's mother that the girl should try to 'exercise through her pain threshold', that the problem was muscular.

Exercise Two

The passage that follows has been divided into seven sections. The first has been printed at the beginning, but the rest have been jumbled up. Study them carefully and work out the correct order. Then write the letters in that order.

A The exploits of RAF pilots who flew in the Battle of Britain or coaxed their damaged Lancasters back from bombing raids over the Ruhr are widely known and have been documented in thousands of volumes of military nostalgia.

B They pressed their case with the authorities, who eventually let them form a small pool of women pilots based at Hatfield, with the arduous task of delivering Tiger Moth training aircraft in winter to RAF flying schools in Scotland.

C What has not been so fully chronicled, however, is the work of the Air Transport Auxiliary, on which, eventually, the entire effort of the war in the air came to depend.

   The ATA was the civilian unit which had to ferry fighters and bombers from the factories to front-line squadrons. Its organization was brilliantly improvised, its task difficult and, in its own way, just as dangerous.

D At first the RAF did not want to have civilian pilots touching their machines at all, let alone women. Articles in the aviation press even suggested that a woman's place should really be elsewhere. But the women pilots in the ATA were all made of strong and influential stuff – many had been flying instructors in the pre-war Civil Air Guard, which Lord Balfour so much admired, and others had friends in high places.

E There were still a few eyebrows raised when some huge bomber touched down on a Lincolnshire airfield, taxied up to the control tower and a woman jumped out. But, soon, because of the desperate pressures of delivering

Spitfires and Hudsons, Mosquitoes and Hurricanes from factories like Eastleigh, near Southampton to dispersal points on camouflaged farms at Marwell and Chattis Hill, the women were totally accepted and shared the same risks as the men.

F The ferry pilots had no escorts or weapons, and there were no radar or navigational aids. But what was even more remarkable was the fact that a significant proportion of the ATA's pilots and engineers were women. Today, more than 40 years on, the women pilots can still recall the male prejudice they often faced when the organization was first persuaded to recruit them.

G The women had to fly the aircraft through freezing temperatures, dropping down for fuel every few hundred miles at (rather surprised) RAF stations, and then somehow return to London by rail warrant, sometimes having to sleep in the luggage-racks of the overcrowded wartime trains.

Soon, of course, the RAF needed aircraft so badly that they could not have spared their own aircrew for ferry duties anyway, and objections about women flying their aircraft disappeared.

If you have answered the last two exercises correctly then you have shown that you can work out the pattern of a piece of writing in your head. Sometimes it is useful to do this working-out more systematically and even to draw a diagram of the pattern you work out. This process involves a number of stages.

1 Thinking about the passage

The comments at the side of this passage represent the thoughts that went through one reader's head as he read.

Introduction: What he feels like (and why) about where they're going.

The training area of 22nd SAS near Hereford is the best place on earth from which to begin a journey up-river into the heart of the jungle. The nearest I had ever come to a tropical rain-forest, after all, was in the Bodleian Library, via the pages of the great nineteenth-century traveller-naturalists, Humboldt, Darwin, Wallace, Bates, Thomas Belt – and, in practice, a childhood spent rabbiting in the Wiltshire woods. My companion, James Fenton, however, whose idea the venture was, enigmatic, balding, an ex-correspondent of the war in Vietnam and Cambodia, a jungle in himself, was a wise old man in these matters.

JF is better prepared - leads into

both unnerved by SAS area

Description, a lot of details

Still, as the gates swung open from a remote control point in the guardroom and our camouflaged Landrover climbed the small track across the fields, even James was unnerved by the view. Boobytrapped lorries and burned-out vehicles littered the landscape; displaced lines of turf disclosed wires running in all directions; from Neolithic-seeming fortressed earthworks, there came the muffled hammering of silenced small-arms fire; impossibly burly hippies in Levi jeans and trendy sweaters piled out of a truck and disappeared into the grass; mock-up streets and shuttered embassies went past, and then, as we drove round a fold in the hill, an airliner appeared, sitting neatly in a field of wheat.

More description

We drew up by a fearsome assault-course and made our way into the local SAS jungle. Apart from the high-wire perimeter fence, the frequency with which Landrovers drove past beyond it, the number of helicopters overhead and the speed with which persons unknown were discharging revolvers from a place whose exact position it was impossible to ascertain, it might have been a wood in England.

joke!
Conversation with SAS man - looks as if this is real beginning of story.

'What a pity,' said Malcolm, our SAS instructor and guide, 'that you can't come to Brunei with us for a week. We could really sort you out and set you up over there.'

'What a pity,' I agreed, moistening with sweat at the very thought.

2 Working out the rough pattern

1. Introduction

2. Description (a)

3. Description (b)

4. Conversation

3 Working out a more detailed pattern

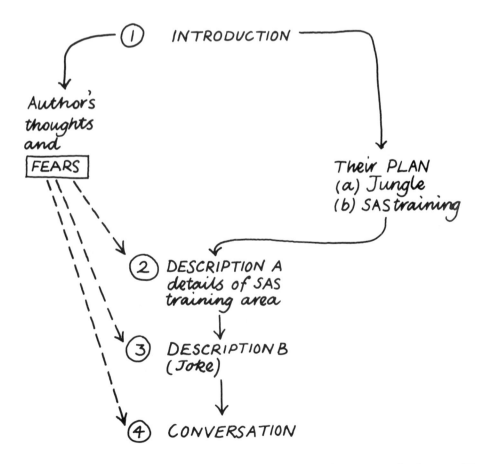

Sorting sentences

When we read a text just once, at speed, we take in only part of the information it contains. Read the passage that follows **once only** and then follow the instructions at the bottom of the page.

Seeing the tall man's long back she thought with a lurch, 'It's like Heneker's back'. Then as he turned round she saw that it was Heneker.

He was standing on a pale strip of sand near the sea, looking down into the cold water, quiet as he had always been, peaceful, unmistakable.

'How *could* it be?' she thought. 'What nonsense! Of course it can't be.'

She went on folding the tee-shirts and jeans, gathering flung sandals, then made two neat heaps with a towel on each, for when the children came out of the sea. She took off her cardigan, pushed her hands back through her hair, gave her face for a moment to the sun; looked again.

She watched her two children run with drumming feet over the hard white strand, splash past the man into the sea, fling themselves in to it in fan of spray, shrieking. Then she looked at the man again.

Long brown legs, long brown back, he was watching with a painter's concentration the movement of the water and the shapes of the children playing in it. Twenty, thirty yards away, yet she could not mistake the slow smile, the acceptance as he narrowed his eyes and looked at lines and planes and shadows that there are wonders on the earth.

It was Heneker all right. Ten years older but decidedly and only Heneker.

He turned, came up the beach, dropped down beside her and said 'Hullo'. He was wearing black swimming trunks and had a beard. 'Funny,' she thought, 'I always laugh at beards in the sea, but he looks all right. He always did look all right. Wherever he was.'

'Hullo,' she said.

Instructions

1   Do not look at the book again.
2   Make a list of the main topics the text is about.
3   Write down as much about each topic as you can remember.

If we want to gain more information then we have to read the text systematically. One way of doing this is to read selectively – to pick out all the sentences that are about a particular aspect of the subject. This text is about three main topics:

    a) what happens
    b) what she sees
    c) what she thinks

Checking

Compare the notes you made with the versions on the facing page.

what happens ➡

Then as he turned round she saw that it was Heneker.
He was standing on a pale strip of sand near the sea, looking down into the cold water,

She went on folding the tee-shirts and jeans, gathering flung sandals, then made two neat heaps with a towel on each, for when the children came out of the sea. She took off her cardigan, pushed her hands back through her hair, gave her face for a moment to the sun; looked again.
She watched her two children run with drumming feet over the hard white strand, splash past the man into the sea, fling themselves in to it in fan of spray, shrieking. Then she looked at the man again.

He turned, came up the beach, dropped down beside her and said 'Hullo'.

'Hullo,' she said.

Seeing the tall man's long back she thought with a lurch, 'It's like Heneker's back'. Then as he turned round she saw that it was Heneker.
He was standing on a pale strip of sand near the sea, looking down into the cold water, quiet as he had always been, peaceful, unmistakable.

Then she looked at the man again.
Long brown legs, long brown back, he was watching with a painter's concentration the movement of the water and the shapes of the children playing in it. Twenty, thirty yards away, yet she could not mistake the slow smile, the acceptance as he narrowed his eyes and looked at lines and planes and shadows that there are wonders on the earth.

He turned, came up the beach, dropped down beside her and said 'Hullo'. He was wearing black swimming trunks and had a beard.

⬅ **what she sees**

---

what she thinks ➡

Seeing the tall man's long back she thought with a lurch, 'It's like Heneker's back'.

'How *could* it be?' she thought. 'What nonsense! Of course it can't be.'

It was Heneker all right. Ten years older but decidedly and only Heneker.

'Funny,' she thought, 'I always laugh at beards in the sea, but he looks all right. He always did look all right. Wherever he was.'

The exercises that follow give practice in the technique of sorting sentences, and then using the information you have discovered, to answer comprehension questions.

Exercise One

The automobile

(1) Even if they are banned from the city, motor vehicles are likely to dominate the short (10–100 mile) range of transportation for a long time to come. (2) There are few men now alive who can remember when it was otherwise; the automobile is so much a part of our existence that it seems hard to believe that it is a child of our century.

(3) Looked at dispassionately, it is an incredible device, which no sane society would tolerate. (4) If any one living before 1900 could have seen the approaches to a modern city on a Monday morning or a Friday evening, he might have imagined that he was in Hell – and he would not be far wrong.

(5) Here we have a situation in which millions of vehicles, each a miracle of (often unnecessary) complication, are hurtling in all directions under the impulse of anything up to 200 horsepower. (6) Many of them are the size of small houses and contain a couple of tons of sophisticated alloys – yet often carry a single passenger. (7) They can travel at 100 mph, but are lucky if they average 20. (8) In one lifetime they have consumed more irreplaceable fuel than has been used in the whole previous history of mankind. (9) The roads to support them, inadequate though they are, cost as much as a small war; the analogy is a good one, for the casualties are on the same scale.

(10) Yet despite the appalling expense in spiritual as well as material values, our civilization could not survive for ten minutes without the automobile.

1 Write down the numbers of all the sentences that tell us about the importance of cars in our lives.
2 Write the numbers of sentences that are about the ways in which cars use energy.
3 Which sentences are about safety?
4 Which sentences are about the disadvantages of cars?
5 Study the lists you have made, then use them to help you answer these questions:
   a) What part, according to the author, does the car play in our lives?
   b) What is his attitude to the ways in which cars make use of energy and other material resources?
   c) What does he have to say about cars and safety?
   d) What other disadvantages of cars does he mention?

Exercise Two

The facts about a theatre company

(1) A typical rehearsal day begins at 9.00 a.m. with Tony Robertson, accompanied by Bach on a cassette in his office, dictating to his secretary the changes he made in the much-changed text at yesterday's rehearsal. (2) Some lines were cut, some were restored. (3) 'I do a rough-cut of the text before we start – obviously the four-hour *Hamlet* is not for us – but I make the final version in rehearsal.'

(4) Shakespeare's text, as finally published in the Folio of 1623, was cut in performance. (5) Two different Quarto versions exist, published in his own lifetime, giving a variety of cuts and the modern director has to pick and choose between the three versions. (6) Typed and bound in the standard form used for film and theatre scripts, stapled into a soft brown cover, it might be a contemporary play – except that the cut-out title window on the front reads *The Tragedy of Hamlet Prince of Denmark*.

(7) On this particular morning, Tony Robertson has had about four hours' sleep, after attending another Prospect opening, of *St. Joan* with a separate company, in Bath the night before. (8) By 10 o'clock the actors are drifting in and assembling in the dressing room behind the stage where instant coffee is dispensed for a 50 pence contribution a week. (9) By 10.30 everyone has climbed the endless backstage stairs to the rehearsal room at the top of the Old Vic for the morning movement class.

(10) This is partly a keep-fit measure, partly a way of training the actors' bodies to move with elegance on the stage. (11) Donald Fraser, the musical director, sits at an old upright piano in the corner while the movement director, William Louther, a former Martha Graham dancer, takes the class.

(12) The company sit cross-legged on the floor in bare feet, wearing headscarves and woolly caps, grasping their ankles, bobbing their foreheads to the ground, rolling their heads to the strains of a Beethoven sonata. (13) It is obvious from their hollow backs which of them are trained dancers. (14) But after a few mornings the class has helped give the company an identity. (15) They have stretched and gasped for breath in unison and it binds them together.

1 Write down the numbers of sentences which are about each of the following topics:
   a) Tony Robertson
   b) The script
   c) The actors
   d) The day's timetable
   e) The movement class
2 Use this information to help you answer the questions that follow, but answer them using your own words as far as possible.
   a) Describe Tony Robertson's job.
   b) What was done to the script of *Hamlet* before the play was rehearsed, and in what ways have changes been made since?
   c) When do the actors arrive and what do they do first?
   d) In what order do things happen throughout the morning?
   e) Why do the actors have a movement class?

Words
Context

When you are reading a passage in detail – as in a comprehension exam – it is easy to be put off when you come across one or two words you don't know. If you met the same words when reading a book or newspaper, they wouldn't worry you at all. You would still understand the gist of what you were reading and even have a general idea of what these new words meant. This is because the **context** in which you read the words gave you clues about their meaning.

Exercise One

Read the passage and then answer the question at the end.

The Dentish army now advanced towards Splek. They were led by the King, followed by the Prince of Wales and a large farble of Dentish nobles. When they reached the village of Splek they gave the order to frimp camp. They were now only one and a half globs from their enemies, the Frungles.

These nonsense words appear in the passage. Think of normal words that you can replace them with so that the passage makes sense.

    Dentish   farble   frimp   globs   Frungles

Exercise Two

Now use the same technique on this passage. The words in **bold** type are unusual but correctly used English words. Try to work out from the context what each one means. Then write one sentence for each word, using it in what you think is the correct way.

The light was fading and we still hadn't found a place to pitch camp. We were following the line of a **holl** which drained the fields on each side. Because the weather had been so hot and dry there was almost no water in the holl and the little water still there was stagnant. So there was a real **hogo** that made you want to hold your nose. Mark started complaining and criticizing Peter for bringing us to this awful place, but I shut him up. I told him that if he didn't **lin** I'd make him. He fell silent straight away.

    Just as it was getting dark we reached the river. We wandered along the bank, looking for a place to camp. Suddenly there was a cry and a lot of splashing: Mark had fallen in. We could just see him, struggling against the current, which at that point was quite strong. Fortunately at that moment a large **shide**, probably broken off from a wooden jetty, was swept along close to Mark and he managed to grab it. It kept him afloat and he managed to make his way to the bank where we hauled him out.

Exercise Three

In the passage that follows a number of words have been missed out. Read the passage carefully and from the context work out what you think the missing words should be. Then write the number of each space and against it write the word you think should fill it.

The Chinese model

China has largely succeeded in eliminating malnutrition – no mean — 1 — in a country that supports one in five of humankind. The Chinese not only produce massive amounts of food, but, – equally to be acclaimed – they — 2 — it is fairly shared among all. Furthermore, they are leaders in 'ecological agriculture', with emphasis on wasting nothing. They — 3 — much of their crop residues and by-products, and also their general garbage and waste (not surprising, when we remember that the Chinese have long had to learn how to make do with — 4 — natural resources).

The largest irrigation network in the world, built at a cost of much human — 5 —, enables China to grow more than one-third of the world's rice, almost as much as the next five together, viz. India, Indonesia, Bangladesh, Japan, and Thailand. Farming — 6 — do not rely on heavy machinery, so that hundreds of millions of peasants are usefully — 7 — on the land. Abundant human labour further allows several crops to be grown in one field in alternate rows, with symbiotic benefit all round (e.g. beans, as legumes, — 8 — 'free' nitrogen fertilizer to wheat plants). Labour-intensive pest control permits crop spraying only against particular outbreaks – a — 9 — that is far more cost-effective and environmentally — 10 — than regular broadscale spraying.

Exercise Four

In this passage, the words that have been missed out are listed at the end, in the wrong order. Read the passage and work out which word should go in which space. Then write the number of each space and beside it the letter of the word you have chosen. Now explain what you think each word means.

A midsummer night's death

Meddington school was housed in a — 1 — Victorian mansion with medieval intentions, the exterior now largely clothed in ivy, the interior lofty, noble and — 2 — cold in winter. In summer it was quite civilized, and Jonathan liked the — 3 — of its towers, buttresses, winding staircases and stone-flagged halls. On some of the knobbly — 4 —, the ivy stripped away, Hugo taught rock-climbing; in one of the towers the music — 5 — practised through long summer evenings to the accompaniment of nesting swallows and mating cuckoos, and in a baronial dining-room the — 6 — clicking of billiard balls and ping-pong echoed in the hammer-beam. A large — 7 — orangery had been converted – in the nineteen-thirties—into a swimming pool, and couched blue and — 8 — beneath a wild tangle of passion-flowers swinging junglewise across the glass roof. Decorated with mosaic floors in the Roman style and smelling to Jonathan strongly of the old Empire, one somehow expected servants to appear with trays of drinks and dry towels. (The river, deep, swift and — 9 —, was severely out of bounds for swimming.) The old place had its — 10 —, but Jonathan always had the feeling that it wasn't part of the real world at all.

eccentricity   maestros   ornate   rambling   treacherous
excruciatingly   façades   enticing   felicities   spasmodic

Words
Similarities

When we are trying to work out the meaning of a word, context is not the only clue we can use. Sometimes we can make use of the fact that there are **similarities** between the word we do not know and a word or words that we do know. The next two exercises give practice in this technique.

Exercise Five

In the passage that follows a number of words are printed in **bold** type. At the bottom of the passage a number of related words are printed with definitions. Use these clues and the clues of context to work out definitions of the words in bold type.

The fragile miracle

The sphere of rock on which we live **coalesced** from the dust of ancient stars. Orbiting round the huge hydrogen furnace of the sun, bathed by **radiant** energy and the solar wind, the globe is white hot and molten beneath the crust: continents ride in a slow dance across its face, ocean floors spread. And between its dynamic surface and the vacuum of space, in a film as thin and **vibrant** as a spider's web, lies the fragile miracle we call the **biosphere**.

When the first astronauts circled the Earth in their tiny craft, millions of listeners heard them describe the beauty of this planet, 'like a blue pearl in space', and were caught up in a moment of extraordinary human **revelation**. Since then, much has been written about 'Spaceship Earth', on whose **finite** resources we all depend. And the more we explore the solar system, the more singular we understand our world to be. The atmospheric mix of gases, for instance, is entirely different not only from that of nearby planets but from what would be predicted by Earth's own chemistry. This 'improbable' state of affairs appears to have arisen alongside the evolution of life, and persisted (with minor fluctuations) despite all possible accidental **perturbations** of cosmic travel, for perhaps two billion years. Life, by its very presence, is apparently creating, and maintaining, the special conditions necessary for its own survival.

It was a group of space scientists devising life-detection experiments for other planets who first stumbled on this phenomenon of the self-sustaining biosphere – and named it Gaia, the living planet. Since then, we have begun to learn much more about the planetary life-support systems which rule our lives – sadly, mainly by disturbing them.

coalition: combination of two or more things
radiate: to emit or give off energy
vibrate: shake, quiver, tremble
biology: study of living organisms
reveal: show
finish: end
perturb: upset

Exercise Six

In this exercise you are on your own. Ten words are printed in bold type. Use the techniques you have learned in this unit to help you work out the meaning of each word *as it is used in the passage.*

After the minibus had departed for Wales, Iris went to her room, threw herself on the bed and sobbed bitterly. Not only was she in despair about being left at Meddington after breaking-up, but her sheer **monumental ineptitude** in the tender region of human relationships was an enduring misery. Would she ever learn? The vision of Jonathan's **bleak**, desperate embarrassment seared her. To have exposed him to her hysteria in front of his friends like that was unforgiveable, and yet she had not foreseen the obvious when she had run after him. She wept, hot with shame.

She could see Jane Reeves in such a **predicament** being cool and tragic and heart-melting, with everyone sympathetic and admiring. Why couldn't she learn? God knows, she had had enough experience of embarrassing and unfortunate situations in the last couple of years to have at least learned the virtues of mere silence ... but then Jane had said silence was **inhibiting**: one shouldn't bottle up one's **innermost** feelings. One must put out feelers, searching for **response**, for meaningful relationship. But she had put out bloody tentacles like an octopus and strangled Meredith almost to death.

She had felt in the past that life had come to a low **ebb**, but never quite so low as this. Even when Robin had died. After all, Robin had been a dream, and one eventually woke up from dreams, but Jonathan wasn't a dream, and would reappear in the flesh in two days' time and no doubt go red as a pillar-box when he set eyes on her again. She had only been driven to approach him because she had sensed in him, somewhere under his **reserve**, an **essential** understanding of her loneliness. In a strange way, he was a lone person too, although highly regarded by just about everybody. Everybody liked him, yet he was close to no one.

3. *Reading between the lines*

Facts, opinions, arguments

When we are reading non-fiction, it is useful to be aware of whether the text is fact, opinion, or argument. Sometimes this is fairly obvious:

Fact   At present there are 1102 pupils in the school, of whom 580 are girls.
Opinion   I think all schools should be mixed.
Argument   Girls and boys should be treated equally in school, because there is no evidence to show that they have different abilities.

A factual statement is one which can be checked against the evidence and about which people should be able to agree.
An opinion expresses a personal belief which the author does not necessarily give reasons for.
In expressing **an argument**, the author gives reasons for the view expressed. These reasons are either facts or are based on facts.

It isn't always as clear as this. There are two main ways in which the author can mislead the reader:

By expressing an opinion as if it were a fact

It's a well-known fact that boys are stronger than girls.

By expressing an opinion as if it were an argument
This is usually done by giving fake 'reasons', which aren't reasons at all, just more opinions.

Women live longer than men because men have to work so much harder than women.

If a writer tries to mislead us in this way, we need to be aware of it. Otherwise we may be fooled into thinking that his/her opinions and prejudices are 'facts'.

Exercise One

For each of the following short texts, state whether it is:
    fact
    opinion
    argument
    opinion pretending to be something else

A   The train left the station at 10.37 and began its journey to Glasgow in the normal way. It picked up speed and started on the slow descent out of town. It was only when it had reached a speed of approximately 45 mph that the driver observed that something was wrong with the braking system.

B   Everybody knows that the country's rail system needs a radical improvement. I never travel by rail myself and I don't know anybody who does – from choice.

C   The railways are logically the best way of moving heavy goods from one part of the country to another, when speed is not important. They are relatively economical in their use of fuel when the items carried weigh a lot; they connect all the major areas which are likely to need this service; when they carry heavy goods it does not disrupt the rest of the system (as it does when a large load is carried by lorry along narrow trunk roads).

D   It's quite obvious that he's not to be trusted. He has a very shifty-looking face and he never looks you in the eye when he's talking to you. No one in their senses would believe a word he's saying. He's certainly not the kind of boy I want my daughter to be seen out with.

E   It isn't easy to give you the information you ask for. I would say I'm an easy-going sort of person and a good mixer. I'm not particularly brainy or good at school things, but I'm certainly not stupid, either.

Exercise Two

Comment on the passage that follows. Is it fact, opinion, or argument? How convincing do you find it and why?

Spain, a Greek island, somewhere even more exotic: any time now it'll be time to pack up your troubles and take off on holiday. The idea of it is marvellous. In practice, it can be a bit of a nightmare, travelling with an old suitcase crammed to zip-bursting point, the family's belongings overflowing into half a dozen shopping bags. ('Mummy, I think I've lost my teddy!')

This year, get your dream holiday right from the start with John Harvey's superb travel set: three matching suitcases with room and to spare for all the family's things – and at a price you'll hardly believe: just £34.95 the three!

Tone

A

B

Both people want the same thing, but they go about it in very different ways. They use a different **tone**. **A** knows the person being addressed very well, and so uses an informal tone. **B** has probably never met the person addressed. The tone used is very formal.

How tone works

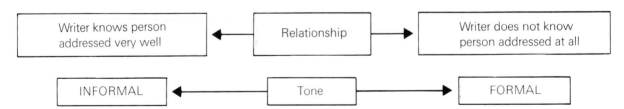

There are other ways in which the tone of a piece of writing can change. It often depends on **the effect that the writer wants to have** on the reader. For example s/he may want to be friendly:

'... so it would be marvellous if you could come with us ...'

or off-hand:

'... and it's up to you whether you feel like coming along ...'

or even threatening:

'... and if you don't come, I shall tell David that ...'

Exercise One

Each of the pairs of texts that follow is about a similar subject but uses a different tone. After each pair there is a list of words that could be used to describe the tone of the writing. Choose words from the list to describe the tone of each passage.

A **1** Helen has not found this subject at all easy. Despite her difficulties, however, she has tried hard and is always cheerful. Although I cannot be confident about success, I am hopeful – she certainly deserves to succeed.

   2 She's not a natural linguist – and she realizes it. Tries hard sometimes.

   unhelpful   enthusiastic   encouraging   hostile   dull

B **1** When you get to the roundabout you've got a choice – you can either go straight across (well, not literally, of course!), or you can take the last exit and follow the road down through Holdenham. It's a bit longer, this one, but more fun, if only because you have to go past old Rhubarb-and-custard's house – well, whatever turns you on!

   2 On reaching the roundabout, take the second exit, signposted Brainton. This road continues fairly straight for about two miles. As you enter Brainton, look for a shop called Timpsons. Fifty yards past this, on the left there is a narrow lane, called The Twitchell. Turn along this and at the end you will see the house.

   official   formal   chatty   off-hand   unemotional

Exercise Two

The texts that follow are also in pairs and show different tones. This time write one or two sentences about each passage describing what you think its tone is and what makes you think so.

C **1** As I left the road and began to make my way across country, I was struck by the immense and desolate flatness of the terrain. All was even, level, drear. The levelness of the land was reflected in the grey unbroken nature of the sky. Not a hill, not a cloud anywhere in sight to break the dull plodding monotony of nature.

   2 The car moved off down the road and I was alone. Alone at last and free. I looked around the vast horizon – nothing. What a feeling of ease and happiness swept through me as I realized I had this enormous rolling plain all to myself! I strode forward, full of joyous anticipation.

D **1** The play was performed in a style that was lively and energetic. The actors showed enormous enthusiasm and great liveliness and pace. For sheer entertainment value I cannot think of a show at present on in the West End to compare with it.

   2 The actors seemed to go crazy, throwing themselves all over the stage in an attempt to breathe life into a script that ranged from the unimaginative to the stupid. The production was frantic and busy, which only went to show that those concerned had mistaken activity for thought. Very disappointing.

Making deductions

When we read we often make deductions from the words on the page. In fact writers usually expect it. They hope we will work things out for ourselves. Some writers even **make** us do it. The passage that follows is the beginning of a short story.

'Venice!' she said, getting up, crossing the room. 'Of course! The Doge's Palace and the Campanile. It's nice. Where did you get it?'

'I saw it in a junk shop.'

London traffic rumbled beyond the window. 'Yes,' she went on. 'Doesn't it take you back! We went over to that church once, the picture must have been done from that side. San – San . . .'

'Santa Maria della Salute.'

'That's it.' She stabbed a finger on the glass. 'That's where I bought the fluorescent necklace. There – under that arch.'

He peered. . . .

Here the writer throws us in at the deep end. We are in the middle of a conversation and we aren't told **who** the people are, **where** they are or **what's** going on. We are left to work it out:

'Venice!' she said, getting up, crossing the room.

From this we can work out:

1 At the beginning of the story a woman, or girl is sitting down indoors.
2 She's having a conversation (or talking to herself).

'Of course!' The Doge's Palace and the Campanile. It's nice. Where did you get it?'

3 There **is** another person in the room.
4 They're talking about something that reminds her of Venice – probably a picture.
5 She has been to Venice, or knows a bit about it.

'I saw it in a junk shop.'

6 The person she is talking to has enough time and money to be able to look round junk shops.

London traffic rumbled beyond the window.

7 The house or flat is in London, near a busy road.

'Yes,' she went on. 'Doesn't it take you back! We went over to that church once, the picture must have been done from that side. San – San . . .'

8 She has visited Venice, some time ago.
9 She enjoyed it. ('Doesn't it take you back!')
10 She probably went with the other person. (We went . . .')

'Santa Maria della Salute.'

'That's it.' She stabbed a finger on the glass. 'That's where I bought the fluorescent necklace. There – under that arch.'

11   It is a picture, in a frame with glass.
12   She is a fairly energetic, active person.
13   She likes bright things.

'He peered . . .'

14   The other person is a man.

We have only read 89 words, yet we have already deduced a lot of information and are beginning to get 'inside' the story.

Fiction

Exercise One

The following passage comes from the beginning of a short story. Read it carefully and then make a list of the information you can deduce from it.

She was crying again last night and that made it easier for me this morning.

I said, 'I'm having lunch with Ruth Sykes today, dear.'

'Mmmm,' she said, black coffee in one hand, toast in the other, peering down at the morning paper laid all across the kitchen table – she never sits down at breakfast.

'So you'll be all right, dear?'

'Mmmm.'

'For lunch I mean – after surgery. I'll leave it ready in the oven. Just to take out.'

'What?'

'Your lunch, dear. After surgery. And your visits. It'll be in the oven.'

She looked at me through her big glasses – such a big, handsome daughter. How could such a great big woman have come out of me? I'm so small. Jack was small, too. And neither of us was anything much. Certainly nothing so clever as a doctor in either of the families, anywhere. It's funny – I look at her, my daughter, my Rosalind and I can't believe she's the same as the baby I had: the fat little round warm bright-eyed thing holding its wrists up in the pram against the light, carefully watching the leaves moving in the birch tree like a peaceful little cat. She's so bold and brave and strong now – fast car, doctor's bag slung in the back, stethoscope, white coat. So quick on the telephone. Oh it's wonderful to hear her on the telephone! – 'Yes? When was this? All right – do nothing until I'm there. I'll be with you in ten minutes.' Oh the lives she must save! She's a wonderful doctor.

But the crying is awful. It was really awful last night.

Fact

It is also useful to make deductions from non-fiction texts. Sometimes this process is similar to that used with fiction texts. The reader has to work like a detective uncovering information:

Exercise Two

Read the passsage that follows and then answer the question after it.

The man they arrested had been living alone in a tumbledown shack near the railway sidings. When they searched it the police found a scene of unbelievable squalor. On a table in a corner stood a dirty plastic basin piled with unwashed plates, cutlery and empty baked bean tins. On the floor beneath it was a litter of lager cans and an empty scotch bottle. A large bucket by the door was almost full of rubbish, mostly cigarette ends, used matches and dated copies of the Sporting Times. On a table in the centre of the room there was another copy of this newspaper with certain horses' names ringed in pencil (a pencil stub lay on top of the paper). Over all hung the smell of unwashed humanity and dirty clothing.

What can you work out about the man who had been living in the shack?

The same kind of reasoning process can be used on other factual texts.

Exercise Three

The questions that follow relate to the text on the facing page. Read it carefully and then work out the answers to the questions.

1 MI5 suspect Ann Hargreaves of being a spy. They question her about her movements on 15th May and she insists that she has spent the day with a friend who lives in Bristol. The friend confirms this. In fact Ann Hargreaves started the day in London where she drove her car past a demonstration outside the American Embassy. She then drove to Colchester, where she bought petrol using a Barclaycard.
   How much of this could MI5 find out using their computer?
2 In the future certain changes will take place to increase the information available to the authorities. How much would MI5 then be able to find out about the man described below by using MOD-X?

He telephoned a contact in Paris and spoke to him for 10 minutes. He then took his car through the Dartford Tunnel (where traffic is monitored by police TV cameras) filled up with petrol in Canterbury (using a credit card) and then proceeded to Dover where he bought a ferry ticket and showed his new passport to an Immigration Officer before getting on to the ferry. Later in the day when he had arrived in Paris he 'phoned a friend in Portsmouth.

CITIZENWATCH

All sorts of Government and private organizations have—or can get—information about you. Much of it is on computer; linked together, such data would provide an extremely detailed picture of your daily life. Some key examples are shown below.

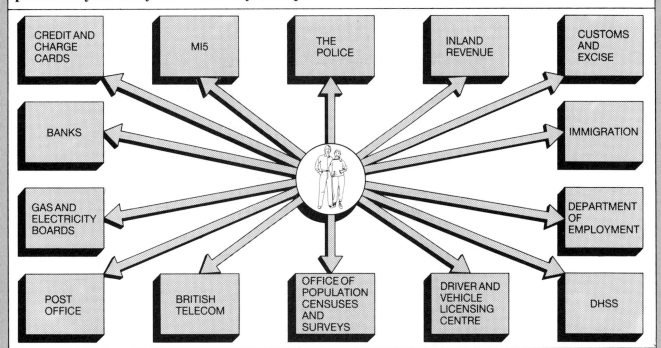

MI5 (Government secret security service) can request—as from 1984—virtually any computer information from police, Immigration, Office of Population, Censuses and Surveys, DHSS, Department of Employment, Inland Revenue, British Telecom, banks, credit cards or any of the 200 'data bases' in Government hands. MI5 keep extensive records of known political activists. They now have an extremely large computer, called MOD-X, based at Mount Street Mayfair, twice the size of the police national computer.

THE POLICE can obtain information from the Post Office, British Telecom, Immigration, banks, credit cards, DVLC, gas and electricity boards. The police increasingly use computers. There is the National Computer at Hendon, which has criminal records on it and direct access to DVLC. Scotland Yard has 'C' Department computer which is used by specialist squads like Special Branch and Immigration. There are a number of experiments in putting collated 'soft' information—often just gossip—on to computers. Police cameras are now used to read car number-plates on key routes. Photographers and roof-top video cameras record demonstrations.

INLAND REVENUE keep much PAYE information on computer and have very detailed personal files on every taxpayer. They have wide powers of search and seizure.

CUSTOMS & EXCISE keep details and records of any VAT-registered business and those exporting or importing goods. They also have an investigation branch, to do with smuggling.

IMMIGRATION 'Machine-readable passports' are planned to be introduced throughout Europe. Immigration men simply have to slip your passport into a machine which will read coded electronic information invisible to the passport's owner. Linked into other computers, this will give an instantaneous permanent record of the individual's travels throughout Europe, and contain information about, for example, alleged political activities.

DEPARTMENT OF EMPLOYMENT holds computerised records for unemployment benefits.

DHSS Much social security information is kept on computer. There is also an increasing trend to computerise medical records which could include sensitive information on abortions, venereal diseases etc.

DRIVER VEHICLE LICENSING CENTRE provides computerised details of cars, owners and addresses to police. Information available in seconds to computer terminals in police stations.

OFFICE OF POPULATION, CENSUSES AND SURVEYS The census reveals personal details of household occupancy—much of this data is computerised (anonymously, it is claimed).

BRITISH TELECOM Besides making phone-tapping easier, System X, new micro-chip telephone exchanges, will be capable of providing itemised computerised bills showing numbers called and duration of calls.

POST OFFICE provides a mail interception service for the police.

GAS AND ELECTRICITY BOARDS now do accounts by computer. Such information can reveal changing patterns in a house—showing when in use and when not, and how many people likely to be living there.

BANKS have discretion as to when to release details of transactions. If banks refuse, various Government agencies can obtain a court order for statements etc. to be turned over to them. Legal judgements indicate that this should be done only when a 'higher public interest' than the privacy of the individual is involved.

CREDIT AND CHARGE CARDS. Both types of card provide vivid diary-like details of an individual's financial transactions. Credit cards are, in effect, another bank account and subject to the same procedures. Charge companies like American Express and Diners Club say they will only release details under a court order.

Generalizing

You sometimes hear people say in an argument 'Oh, you can't generalize'. But in life not only can we generalize but often we must. It saves time and helps us run our lives. Look at the following tables and then answer the questions at the end.

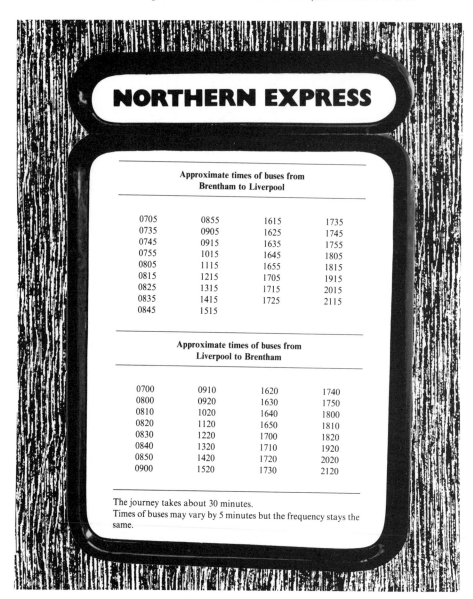

NORTHERN EXPRESS

Approximate times of buses from Brentham to Liverpool

0705	0855	1615	1735
0735	0905	1625	1745
0745	0915	1635	1755
0755	1015	1645	1805
0805	1115	1655	1815
0815	1215	1705	1915
0825	1315	1715	2015
0835	1415	1725	2115
0845	1515		

Approximate times of buses from Liverpool to Brentham

0700	0910	1620	1740
0800	0920	1630	1750
0810	1020	1640	1800
0820	1120	1650	1810
0830	1220	1700	1820
0840	1320	1710	1920
0850	1420	1720	2020
0900	1520	1730	2120

The journey takes about 30 minutes.
Times of buses may vary by 5 minutes but the frequency stays the same.

Exercise One

You want to travel from Brentham to Liverpool and spend most of the day there before returning. You don't want to hang around waiting for a bus. When would be the best period of the day to travel a) from Brentham to Liverpool b) back from Liverpool?

You can only answer this question by generalizing. The same process helps us to make sense of passages of writing as well.

Exercise Two

Read the text that follows and then answer the questions.

The story concerns four strange beings from the land of Zora. Ando lives in the village of Edmorph and her favourite food is Gruyère cheese. She is into her twelfth year and her favourite spare time activity is knitting. Barshen lives in Flon and likes hazelnuts. She is into her twelfth year and likes knitting. Cadrin is just six and likes Gruyère cheese. She lives in Edmorph and enjoys Lego. Dentak who is just six is a Lego fan. She likes hazelnuts and lives in Flon. I live in Flon and enjoy knitting.

1   What is my favourite food likely to be?
2   How old am I likely to be?
3   How do you know?

Hint: If you find the problem difficult, copy and complete the following table:

Name	Home	Food	Age	Activity
Ando Barshen Cadrin Dentak	Edmorph	Gruyère	11+	knitting

Exercise Three

This passage is an extract from an article about vandalism. Read it carefully and then answer the questions that follow it.

Vandalism costs Britain £100 million a year. Some of that money goes to repair damage. An increasing amount goes to buy 'vandal-proof' materials. Indeed, firms making vandal-proof metal and windows are doing a roaring trade. These firms sell polycarbonate glazing which costs three times more than normal glass but pays for itself by resisting attack and discouraging would-be destroyers. One firm has developed a vandal-proof street sign. The surface can be scratched or dented, but the name shows clearly through. Aerosol spray lettering can be removed with meths. Companies which used to concentrate on providing and fitting burglar alarms have now adapted their products to fit public buildings with vandal alarm systems which employ electric ears to detect the presence of aliens whilst ignoring the 'known' noises of the buildings.

But it will take years before this technology can protect all areas at risk, particularly now that every public body has to make cuts in its spending. What do we know about vandals? What makes someone commit an act of vandalism? Vandalism usually attracts teenage boys who will not later be tempted to lead lives of crime. It is a phase which many boys have to go through. Therefore, to talk of corporal punishment, detention centres or labour camps for them is almost as crazy as talking about tactical nuclear weapons to defeat the IRA. On the other hand, to say that vandalism is the fault of the environment and the homes where children have been brought up does not help much. We simply do not know how much multi-storey flats, over-large estates or homes in which both mother and father work, sometimes returning home late, contribute to vandalism.

If none of the theories about the causes of vandalism is fool-proof, we have to return to prevention, based upon what we know of the kind of targets vandals attack, when they attack and the conditions that favour their attacks. Vandals attack schools but mainly when the schools are empty at night or during holidays. They attack derelict or empty housing. They attack lifts in multi-storey flats or car parks and other enclosed areas where acts can be performed in private. They write on the upper decks of buses away from the one-man operators. So, we ought to let people use places like schools outside school hours and, failing that, to guard them twenty-four hours a day, surely, cheaper than the present £20 million per year schools' repair bill. Tenants' and residents' associations can be highly effective, too. Unlike the police, their members are always around and have a direct personal stake in stopping vandals. British Telecom has given a lead. To prevent vandalism of telephone kiosks it has invited local communities to 'adopt a phone box'. Because it is annoying to find a kiosk out of order British Telecom's lead has met with a good response.

1　Each of the three paragraphs is about a different aspect of the problem of vandalism. Give each one a title.
2　Which paragraph contains information about each of the following topics?:
　　a)　How ordinary citizens can help combat vandalism
　　b)　Why young people commit acts of vandalism
　　c)　How 'vandal-proofing' can be built in where a building is being constructed
3　Write one sentence for each paragraph summing up what it is about.

The energy-efficient house

Saving energy

The fuel misers The energy efficiency of tomorrow's average house and car will be dramatically better than for their 1960 counterparts.

Solar panels installed on the roof, can significantly cut fuel bills for heat and electricity—particularly when coupled with new heat storage and distribution systems.

Insulation is now built into most new houses, both in roof-space and cavity walls. Coupled with double-glazing, such methods significantly cut the energy needed to keep a northern house comfortable from the current requirement of 12–20 kilowatts to an efficient and cost-effective 5 kilowatts.

Building in intelligence can help improve the efficiency of all energy-consuming systems, whether they be entire houses (with thermostats controlling temperatures) or individual items of domestic equipment. By using advanced microelectronics, it will soon be possible for the electricity-supply utility to keep energy-consuming equipment in each household constantly informed of the present price of electricity being supplied.

Improved car design has already turned yesterday's gas guzzlers into today's lighter, sleeker vehicles. But the fuel consumption of even the latest cars could be halved with the use of more plastics in bodywork, more ceramic components in the engine, and microprocessor-based fuel-management systems.

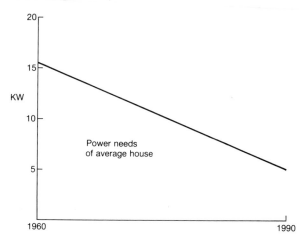

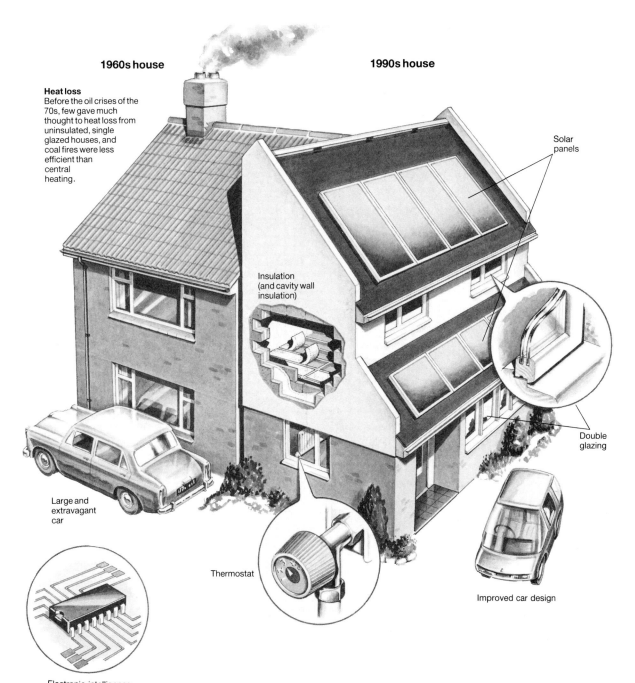

1960s house

1990s house

Heat loss
Before the oil crises of the 70s, few gave much thought to heat loss from uninsulated, single glazed houses, and coal fires were less efficient than central heating.

Solar panels

Insulation (and cavity wall insulation)

Double glazing

Large and extravagant car

Thermostat

Improved car design

Electronic intelligence

Exercise Four

The information on these two pages is presented in a number of different ways – and information about one topic may be found in more than one place.

1 Study the information on *Saving energy* carefully.
2 Find all the information about each of the following topics:
   a) How energy can be saved by preventing heat loss
   b) Other ways in which the amount of fuel used can be reduced.
3 Make notes on each of these topics.
4 Write a paragraph of 50–100 words about each topic.

Section B: Non-literary texts

1. Introductory units

2. Transitional units

3. Test units

1. *Introductory units*

Termites

Termites occur very widely throughout the world. They are generally regarded as a serious nuisance and would seem to have very few friends. Yet this is not altogether the case. If you drive along a road in East Africa at certain times of the year, you may be intrigued to see little green mounds on the verge. Those shallow mounds at the roadside are termite traps – supple green branches and twigs pegged down to make a cool and humid space to encourage the termites to fly. In the rainy season as the heat of the African day leaves the soil, many millions of termites fly out, as over a wide area all the nests of a given species swarm simultaneously before mating. It looks briefly like a blizzard turned upside-down, but the large white wings break off as the insects land, and now they must run about searching for a mate. In this state they are an easy prey for the country people who have located the

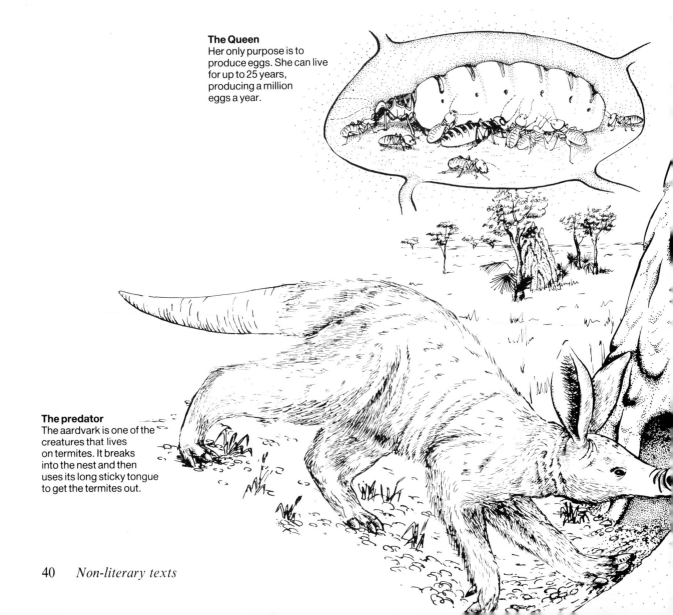

The Queen
Her only purpose is to produce eggs. She can live for up to 25 years, producing a million eggs a year.

The predator
The aardvark is one of the creatures that lives on termites. It breaks into the nest and then uses its long sticky tongue to get the termites out.

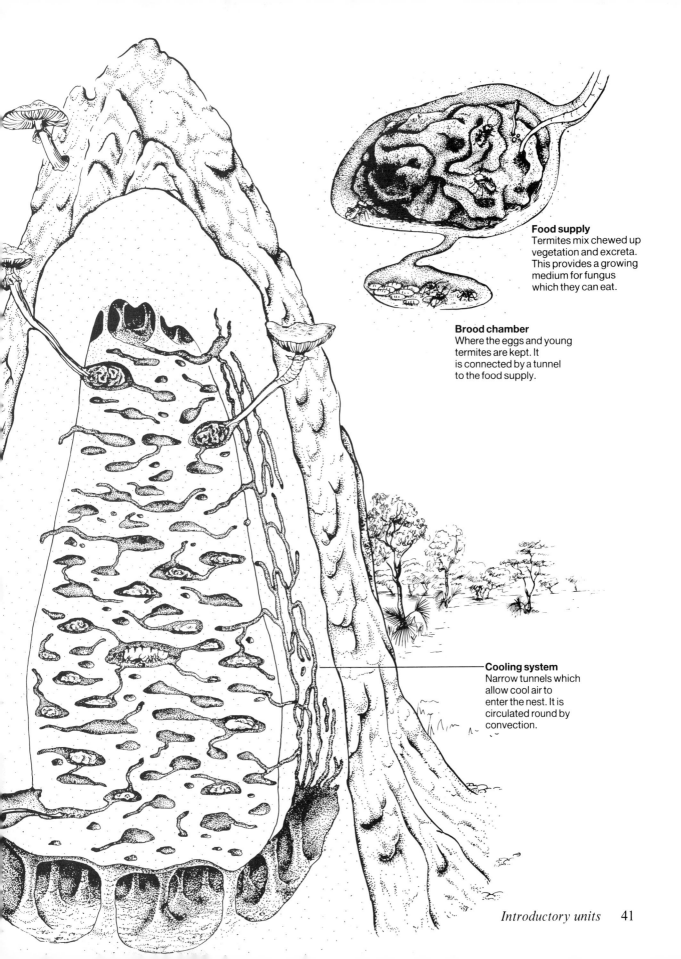

Food supply
Termites mix chewed up vegetation and excreta. This provides a growing medium for fungus which they can eat.

Brood chamber
Where the eggs and young termites are kept. It is connected by a tunnel to the food supply.

Cooling system
Narrow tunnels which allow cool air to enter the nest. It is circulated round by convection.

nest and eat the creatures raw or take them away to eat later, dried and fried.

These termites are well-supplied with fat and protein in order to start new colonies without having to leave the shelter of the new nest to forage. So they are a rich source of nourishing food for an enormous range of predators, including, in addition to humans, mammals such as the ant bear or aardvark and the ant wolf, which with its sticky tongue can consume some 40,000 termites in three hours of feeding. Other creatures happy to gorge themselves on termites include baboons and monkeys, hedgehogs, shrews, vultures, storks, buzzards, falcons, shrikes, glossy starlings, eagle owls, nightjars, bats, geckos, toads, crabs, scorpions, spiders, frogs and ants. Large predatory ants known as stink ants, hunt termites individually. The smaller, equally fierce, ponerine ants go out hunting in an organized manner, in columns of up to 300; they return from their raids still in column, each ant carrying a termite in its jaws.

Termites occur wherever there are trees, for most feed on dead wood. In the bush they consume all the acacias which have been knocked over and killed by elephants, and the resulting humus and organic material enrich the soil. They can eat wood because they have in their intestines microscopic

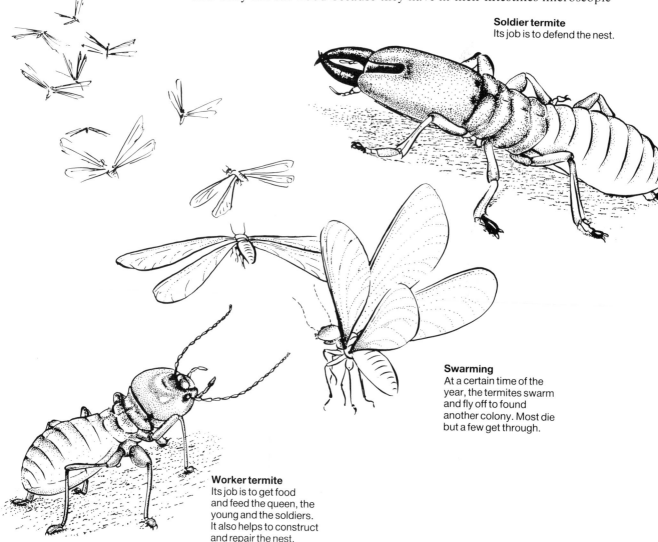

Soldier termite
Its job is to defend the nest.

Swarming
At a certain time of the year, the termites swarm and fly off to found another colony. Most die but a few get through.

Worker termite
Its job is to get food and feed the queen, the young and the soldiers. It also helps to construct and repair the nest.

protozoa which break down cellulose, turning it into sugar. Unfortunately timber houses and farm buildings, furniture, telephone poles, ships and guns are just some of the items which count as dead wood to the termite hordes which munch their way steadily through them, leaving a fragile outer shell to collapse at last. Others do not eat wood at all but instead cultivate fungi for food inside their termite mounds. These are tall reddish towers which may reach a height of over 4 metres and are a striking feature of the bush landscape. The tower walls are plaster-hard and solid, made of soil and small pieces of grass, bound together by special, dry, hard termite excrement. The main termite nests are in the ground beneath the towers, swarming with the intricate organization of workers, white nymphs and soldiers. The termite civilization has been described as 'the most complex, the most intelligent, the most logical and best fitted to the difficulties of existence on this planet'.

Introductory work: text and illustrations

1. Go through the stages of 'the reading route' (p. 12) and make sure that you can answer all the questions.
2. Work out which sentences provide information about each of these topics:
   a) What happens when termites swarm
   b) Creatures that eat termites
   c) How termites eat and digest wood
   d) How termites cause damage
   e) Different kinds of termites
   f) Termite nests
3. Write **brief** notes on each of the topics listed in question 2.
4. Draw a diagram illustrating the **pattern** of the text. (If you are not sure how to do this, look at pp. 14–17.)
5. Make a list of words that you are not sure of. Use the context to help you work out their meaning. (See pp. 22–25.)

Questions

1. Explain in your own words how a termite trap works.
2. Why do termites swarm?
3. Why are swarming termites so attractive to the creatures that eat them?
4. How do ant-wolves catch termites?
5. What is the difference in the hunting methods of the stink ants and the ponerine ants?
6. How are termites able to digest the cellulose in wood?
7. The fact that termites eat dead wood is both useful and harmful. Give one example of its usefulness and one example of its harmfulness.
8. What are termite nests made of?
9. How do termites ensure a supply of fresh air in their nests?
10. What are the main differences between a soldier termite and a worker termite?

Directed writing

Use the information in the passage and pictures to write a short article for an information book for young children. Write on the theme of 'The termite: man's enemy and friend'. Write about 100 words.

'I can't even boil an egg!'

The trouble is that males have long been conditioned to believe that they are somehow free of domestic responsibility, even if the woman of the household works outside the home. I remember a girl who was about to take O levels saying to me bitterly during a class discussion, 'Exams or not, Mum still expects me to help wash and get the meals every evening, and make my own bed. But if my brother as much as puts a plate on the table everyone falls about in admiration!' And it is true that men usually feel very noble indeed if they perform a few simple chores, always on the assumption that it isn't really their job, after all. 'Did you notice I'd taken your rubbish to the dustbin?' one husband asked his wife, seeking praise. And she replied, 'Well, I could say thank you – but tell me just why is it all **my** rubbish in this little home we share and equally mess up?'

Because boys are often not taught the basics of keeping a home going or made to feel any responsibility for it, they can always plead incompetence in later life – which is an easy way to slide out of things. The philosopher A. J. Ayer once described his domestic arrangements in a newspaper interview: 'I've changed Nicholas's (his son's) nappies in a crisis. I am not in fact very helpful round the house – not at all out of principle, simply because I'm not very good at it. It doesn't come naturally. I learned how to make a bed in the army. I have been washing up recently, rather incompetently. I can't cook, I'm afraid. I can cook an egg. In a sense my wife sort of runs Nicholas. She's much more of a managing character than I am. She tends to take the day-to-day decisions ... I think that's true of most households, don't you think?'

It is a sorry comment on the built-in bias of our social education that a man as highly intelligent as Ayer can admit quite unashamedly in public that he can't even wash up properly or cook a simple meal; the assumption being, of course, that such tedious chores **do** 'come naturally' to women. As

novelist Margaret Drabble crisply put it, 'I no longer find it touching or amusing when men say they do not know how to boil an egg. I think it damn silly.' For, she continued, eating is one of the most fundamental processes of human survival, and **not** to teach boys how to prepare their own food is actually handicapping them by making them forever dependent on someone else – invariably a woman – to do it for them.

Pat Barr   *The Framing of the Female*

Introductory work

1   Go through the stages of the reading route (p. 12) and answer (in your head) as many of the questions as you can. Now write two or three sentences explaining what kind of text this is and what its purpose and audience are.
2   The passage contains three paragraphs. For each one write one sentence saying what you think it is about.
3   Draw a diagram to show the main pattern of this text. (See pp. 16–17.)
4   Use sentence sorting (pp. 18–21) to find all the sentences on these topics:
    a)   The way boys and girls are treated in the family
    b)   The responsibility of education
    c)   Examples of men's feebleness in the home
    d)   Examples of women having to do all the housework
5   Is this text (a) opinion, (b) argument, or (c) a mixture of opinion and argument? (See pp. 26–27 if you are not sure of the meaning of these terms.)

Questions

1   The first paragraph includes a complaint by a girl about unequal treatment at home. What is her complaint?
2   Explain the point of the piece of conversation quoted at the end of the first paragraph.
3   At the beginning of the second paragraph it says that 'boys ... can always plead incompetence in later life'.
    a)   What does this mean?
    b)   What reasons are given to explain it?
4   In the third paragraph what is meant by the words 'the built-in bias of our social education'?
5   In what way has Margaret Drabble's view of male attitudes changed?
6   Why are boys being handicapped if they aren't taught to prepare their own food?
7   From this passage it is clear that the writer has fairly strong views on (a) the treatment of boys at home and (b) their education. Explain what these views are in 50–75 of your own words.

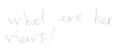

Directed writing

1   Write a conversation between Margaret Drabble and A. J. Ayer about the roles of men and women in society.
2   Write a short essay expressing your own views on this subject.

The Luddites

The early nineteenth century saw the beginning of great industrial changes in England. Machines were beginning to replace craftsmen, a prelude to the factory system. Together with the effects of the Napoleonic wars, and then hostilities with the United States, this caused widespread unemployment and misery. In desperation, gangs of men – called Luddites – broke up many of   5
the 'obnoxious machines', mostly in night attacks. Starting at Arnold, near Nottingham, on March 11, 1811, these acts of violence spread throughout the Midlands, then to Lancashire, Cheshire and the West Riding of Yorkshire. On the night of November 4 the attacks were renewed. Without warning, six frames were wrecked in Bulwell, a village with a population of   10
about two thousand. The spirit of riot flared up again. More outbreaks erupted on the following nights. Machine-wrecking now took an even more dramatic turn. Framework-knitters from Arnold, augmented by others, assembled secretly in Bulwell forest. In military style, they responded to the commands of a man who went under the name of 'General Ludd'.   15
Numbering about seventy, they set off for Bulwell, for the workshop of Edward Hollingsworth, a hosier loathed by the knitters. Hollingsworth, anticipating trouble, had barricaded his windows and doors and planned an armed defence. He had also removed some of his frames to safety in Nottingham. But the nature and ferocity of the attack, carried out with the   20
precision of a military sortie, caught him unawares. The attackers, calling themselves Luddites, were armed as well. Soon shots shattered the night and an Arnold man, John Westley, fell dead. Yet his death merely made the Luddites more tenacious. They compelled the defenders to submit, smashed a number of frames, then quickly dispersed.   25

From then on such attacks were more frequent, and 'Luddism' became a household word. Whenever it was mentioned, it brought to mind bands of rioters organized to destroy machinery. The origin of the name itself is unusual. One version claims that in 1779 there lived in a Leicestershire village a boy called Ned Ludd. He was of weak intellect and became,   30
unfortunately, the butt of other boys. Once, he chased one of his tormentors

into a house, but failed to catch him. In his frustration he attacked two frames which happened to be there. Henceforth, whenever any machines were broken, the breakages were attributed to Ludd. A variant of this tale claims that Ned Ludd was apprenticed to learn framework knitting at Anstey, near Leicester. He was thrashed for laziness and retaliated by hammering his hated frame to pieces. 35

The Luddites signed their proclamations 'Ned Ludd', and sometimes gave Sherwood Forest as their address. One proclamation sent to the Home Office contended that a Charter granted by Charles II to the stocking trade permitted the framework knitters to wreck all machines which made goods in a deceitful manner. Moreover, they could break the frames of hosiers who failed to pay the regular prices agreed to by hosiers and men. Indeed, 'all frames of whatsoever description the workmen of whom are not paid in the current coin of the realm will invariably be destroyed'. At the same time, however, the Luddites denounced any robbery which went on in the course of frame-breaking attacks. 40 45

Douglas Liversidge   *The Luddites* (adapted)

Introductory work

1   This passage consists of three paragraphs. Give each one a title which sums up what it is about.
2   Draw a diagram showing the pattern of thought in the passage. (See pp. 14–17.)
3   Make a list of difficult words. Use the context and other clues to help you work out their meanings. Check your answers in a dictionary.
4   Make a **very brief** list of historical events described in the passage. Write them down in the order in which they happened.

Questions

1   What is 'the factory system'?
2   How was the replacement of craftsmen by machines a 'prelude' to it?
3   Where did the machine-breaking attacks start?
4   'Machine-wrecking now took an even more dramatic turn.' What was 'dramatic' about what happened?
5   From where did the men who attacked Hollingsworth's workshop come?
6   Hollingsworth defended his frames in two different ways. What were they?
7   There are two stories about Ned Ludd, which give different reasons for the event which led to his smashing a frame. Explain **briefly** what these are.
8   The proclamation sent to the Home Office listed three situations in which framework knitters were entitled to smash frames. Explain what these were, using your own words.
9   Explain the meaning of each of the following words and phrases as it is used in the passage:
obnoxious (l. 6)   the spirit of riot (l. 11)   augmented (l. 13)
a military sortie (l. 21)   tenacious (l. 24)   of weak intellect (l. 30)
10   Write a paragraph of about 75 words in which you explain **why** the Luddites smashed machines.

Directed writing

Write a conversation between a hosier like Edward Hollingsworth and a Luddite leader in which each expresses his views about the new machines.

Occupation

I was just 15 when the Germans overran the Netherlands, occupied it, and terrorized it for five years. It was, however, nothing like a 'war' fought on battlefields, or the war as experienced in Britain. It was a personal hatred fought on a personal basis between the Germans and the Dutch; i.e. the Dutch who chose to resist. Privacy or freedom in one's own house, or indeed 5 anywhere else, no longer existed.

I remember having to give up my bicycle on the way to school. The iron was needed to fight the British. I remember later on typing out the news broadcast from London, and distributing it afterwards . . . a highly dangerous activity. 10

There was nothing unusual about the Gestapo entering one's flat and carrying out a search for Jews, or any Jewish belongings. Gestapo 'visits' could happen any time of the day or night. The penalty for their visit proving successful was death.

Perhaps the hardest to get used to was the total lack of freedom in the 15 broadest sense of the word and the sad lack of communication. One's best friends could not be trusted. There was always that risk of their being on the German side for mere material or just plain survival reasons. Communication, except 'underground' became almost non-existent. It became a teenage period spent in bottled up silence with death seemingly as 20 the only reality.

The last winter of 1944–45 brought the greatest suffering, especially for Amsterdam, the capital and the headquarters of the underground forces. The Germans decided to starve us and to deny us all civilized amenities. There was no electricity, no gas, no fuel, no food – and I mean no food whatsoever 25 – and water for only part of the day. This went on from October till May.

That winter turned out to be extremely severe. Snow lay knee deep. Old people and young children died from exhaustion in the streets. By now we had become numb and sadly unshockable. Funerals had long ceased to take place. A label on a toe, and a final ride on a dust cart to a communal grave 30 . . . was all they got.

The Germans had the upper hand. All we were given to eat was a small ration of tulip bulbs. The Dutch, so renowned for their tulips, were now made to eat them. We were starving all right. But still we had hope. Life was

not hard, it simply did not exist any longer. We vegetated and listened $\qquad$ 35
secretly to the BBC. Bedtime was at 4 p.m. when darkness fell.

*   *   *

This may have sounded a sad, pitiful tale of woe. However, in spite of it all, I
sometimes believe that in a perverse sort of way, perhaps we had some
advantages over the teenager of today.

During those cruel long years of occupation in Amsterdam, at least we $\qquad$ 40
had had a definite purpose in our lives: the fight for freedom. We had hope.
We obstinately believed in a better future. Here was a legitimate outlet for
violence and aggression – indeed it was applauded as acts of heroism! We
were never bored – real life was all too dangerously exciting as it was.

I experienced intense fear, domination, humiliation, hunger and pain. I $\qquad$ 45
missed a normal turbulent teenage period altogether. Yet perhaps I have
found out what freedom really is about.

Carla Markham   *The Guardian* May 7, 1985 (edited)

Introductory work

1   The text is in two sections divided by a row of asterisks (***). Explain briefly the
    different subject matter of these two sections.
2   There are ten paragraphs. Give each one a short descriptive title.
3   Make brief notes on each of the following topics:
    Lack of privacy   The winter of 1944–45: lack of food
    Lack of freedom   The winter of 1944–45: the cold
    Lack of trust   The positive things about the occupation

Questions

1   What word in the first paragraph sums up the way the Germans treated the
    Netherlands?
2   Why did the writer lose her bicycle?
3   What happened if the Gestapo found 'Jews or any Jewish belongings' in a
    person's flat?
4   What reasons are suggested for a Dutch person being on the German side?
5   What is meant by 'underground' in paragraph 4?
6   Explain briefly the meaning to the citizens of Amsterdam of the words, 'The
    Germans decided to ...... deny us all civilized amenities'. (I. 24)
7   Write a brief explanation of the meaning of the following words and phrases:
        numb (I. 29)   communal grave (I. 30)   vegetated (I. 35)
        perverse (I. 38)   a legitimate outlet for violence (I. 42)
8   In the last three paragraphs the writer says that there was a positive side to the
    German occupation of the Netherlands. Summarize what she says on this
    subject in not more than 70 words.

Directed writing

In May 1945 Amsterdam was liberated by Canadian forces. You are a teenager living
in Amsterdam at that time. You have a penfriend in England. Write a letter telling
him/her of your thoughts and feelings at the time of liberation.

Fast driving

A

SAAB 900 TURBO 16S · VOTED DIRECTOR'S CAR OF THE YEAR
'UTTERLY THRILLING' · 'UNBELIEVABLY QUICK' · 'ROCKETSHIP ACCELERATION' · 'A JOY TO HURL THROUGH A SERIES OF TIGHT BENDS'
'ALWAYS FEELS VERY SAFE' · QUOTES AND AWARD BY WHAT CAR?
BROCHURES AND DEALER LIST CONTACT (0272) 277666 · OR FREEPOST SAAB · BRISTOL BS1 4YP · EXPORT ENQUIRIES (01) 409 0990

'I HEAR IT'S THE WORLD'S ONLY 16 VALVE TURBO SALOON.'
'NOT QUITE' HE SMILED
'THERE'S A CHAP WITH ONE IN GUILDFORD...'

SAAB
THE AIRCRAFT COMPANY
NOTHING ON EARTH COMES CLOSE.

B **1** When a man climbs into a fast car, he and car become one creature, an updated version of the legendary creature called a centaur which was half man, half horse. Car-man feels that the car's power is his power. Exercising this power gives him confidence in his own strength.

2 Driving a car at high speed appeals to people who lack confidence and feel the need to appear superior to others. The weediest man in a 100 mph (160 km/h) sports car can establish himself as a manly hero in the eyes of an attractive girl. If he feels like a hero, and is regarded as one, he may come to behave like one.

3 Driving very fast, to the public danger, is, in fact, one of the simplest ways for a nobody to feel a somebody. The immediate sense of power and glory which it gives can compensate for many of the frustrations, tensions, failures and disappointments of everyday life. After bickering with his wife or being carpeted by the boss, a man can get his self-esteem back on the road by putting his foot down.

4 This abuse of speed can make a man as dangerous on the road as if he were under the influence of drink. Such a driver, speeding at the very limit of his driving skill, works out his aggression on whatever happens to cross his path. Together with the anger there may well be suicidal self-pity. 'They'll be sorry if I get hurt,' he thinks as he corners too fast. Or: 'They'll wish they'd been kinder when I'm gone'. After a time speed soothes and emotion subsides.

5 Fast driving may also be a relaxation and a joy, taking the mind off trials and tribulations for which the driver knows no remedy. The fast driver won't save much time, but by relaxing in this way he may well be preventing an ulcer. Speed has its own strains and stresses but the man who drives at 80 mph (130 km/h) may find these much less irksome than those which confront him as he paces his office at 2 mph.

6 The ton-up kid in a leather jacket speeding past you on a motor-cycle may have quite a different motive. Young people in industrial Britain feel the age-old need to prove themselves and many drive at 100 mph on a motor-cycle to demonstrate that they have arrived at manhood. The danger shows they are capable of outfacing death, the speed that they are capable of exercising a man's power.

7 Proving manhood by speed is not confined to the young. In psychiatric practice it is found that some people remain emotionally immature all their lives and may feel the need to prove their manhood in middle age. Dangerous speed has fewer attractions for the mature man, who is restrained from courting danger by a sense of responsibility to others.

Introductory work on B

1 Use the reading route on p. 12.
2 Each of these seven sentences sums up one of the paragraphs in the passage. They are in the wrong order. Work out the correct order and write down the number of each paragraph and the letter of the sentence that sums it up.

   a) It's different for the young: they use speed as a way of proving themselves.
   b) But fast driving can also be good for the driver.
   c) This kind of behaviour can be very dangerous.
   d) Some older people never grow up and use speed in a similar way.
   e) A fast car can be a boost to a man's self-confidence.
   f) Driving fast gives a man a sense of power: it makes him feel like the mythical centaur.
   g) Driving fast is a way of making up for your own feelings of weakness in daily life.

Questions on A

1 What are the main features of the SAAB 900 Turbo 16S emphasized by the advertisement? List them and for each one either **quote** from the wording of the advertisement or explain **how** the advertisement conveys this message.
2 What is the point of the three lines beginning 'I hear it's the world's. . . .' and ending '. . . . one in Guildford.'?

Questions on B

1 Why does the writer compare the driver of a fast car to a centaur?
2 How does driving fast help the man who has 'been carpeted by the boss'?
3 How can driving fast prevent an ulcer?
4 Explain in your own words the meanings of the following words and phrases as they are used in the passage:
      to the public danger (para. 3)
      works out his aggression (para. 4)
      irksome (para. 5)
      restrained from courting danger (para. 7)
5 The writer explains in paragraphs 2 and 3 why some people drive fast. In not more than 60 of your own words summarize this explanation.
6 Later the writer suggests some beneficial effects of fast driving. What are they?
7 The last paragraph explains that certain older men have something in common with young people, when it comes to speed. Explain it in not more than 40 of your own words.

Question on A and B

In what ways does the advertisement bear out the comments made by the writer of the article?

Directed writing

Write a short argument expressing the pros and cons of fitting all new cars with a 'governor' that would limit their maximum speed to 55 mph.

Opening a bank account

A

When I go into a bank I get rattled. The clerks rattle me; the cash tills rattle me; the sight of the money rattles me; everything rattles me.

The moment I cross the threshold of a bank and attempt to transact business there, I become an irresponsible idiot.

I knew this beforehand, but my salary had been raised to fifty dollars a month and I felt that the bank was the only place for it. 5

So I shambled in and looked timidly around at the clerks. I had an idea that a person about to open an account must consult the manager.

I went up to a till marked 'Accountant'. The accountant was a tall, cool devil. The very sight of him rattled me. My voice was hollow sounding. 10

'Can I see the manager?' I said, and added solemnly, 'alone'. I don't know why I said 'alone'.

'Certainly,' said the accountant, and fetched him.

The manager was a grave, calm man. I held my fifty-six dollars clutched in a crumpled ball in my pocket. 15

'Are you the manager?' I said. God knows I didn't doubt it.

'Yes,' he said.

'Can I see you,' I asked, 'alone?' I didn't want to say 'alone' again, but without it the thing seemed self-evident.

The manager looked at me in some alarm. He felt that I had some awful 20
secret to reveal.

'Come in here,' he said, and led the way to a private room. He turned the key in the lock.

'We are safe from interruption here,' he said. 'Sit down.'

We both sat down and looked at each other. I found no voice to speak. 25

'You are one of Pinkerton's men, I presume,' he said.

He had gathered from my mysterious manner that I was a detective. I knew what he was thinking, and it made me worse.

'No, not from Pinkerton's,' I said, seeming to imply that I came from a rival agency. 30

'To tell the truth,' I went on, as if I had been prompted to lie about it, 'I am not a detective at all. I have come to open an account. I intend to keep all my money in this bank.'

The manager looked relieved but still serious: he concluded now that I was a son of Baron Rothschild or a young Gould, two of the richest men in 35
America.

'A large account, I suppose,' he said.

'Fairly large,' I whispered. 'I propose to deposit fifty-six dollars now and fifty dollars a month regularly.'

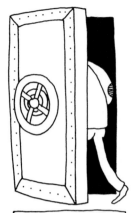

The manager got up and opened the door. He called to the accountant.   40

'Mr Montgomery,' he said unkindly loud, 'this gentleman is opening an account; he will deposit fifty-six dollars. Good morning.'

I rose.

A big iron door stood open at the side of the room.

'Good morning,' I said, and stepped into the safe. 'Come out,' said the   45
manager coldly, and showed me the other way.

I went up to the accountant's desk and poked the ball of money at him with a sudden movement as if I were doing a conjuring trick.

My face was ghastly pale.

'Here,' I said, 'deposit it.' The tone of the words seemed to mean, 'Let us   50
do this painful thing while the fit is on us.'

He took the money and gave it to another clerk.

He made me write the sum on a slip and sign my name in a book. I no longer knew what I was doing. The bank swam before my eyes.

'Is it deposited?' I asked in a hollow, vibrating voice.   55

'It is,' said the accountant.

'Then I want to draw a cheque.'

My idea was to draw out six dollars of it for present use. Someone gave me a cheque book and someone else began telling me how to write it out. The people in the bank had the impression that I was an invalid millionaire.   60
I wrote something on the cheque and thrust it in at the clerk. He looked at it.

'What! Are you drawing it all out again?' He asked in surprise.

Then I realized that I had written fifty-six instead of six. I was too far gone to reason now. I had a feeling that it was impossible to explain the thing. All the clerks had stopped writing to look at me.   65

Reckless with misery, I made a plunge.

'Yes, the whole thing.'

'You want to withdraw your money from the bank?'

'Every cent of it.'

'Are you not going to deposit any more?' said the clerk, astonished.   70

'Never.'

An idiot hope struck me that they might think something had insulted me while I was writing the cheque and that I had changed my mind. I made a wretched attempt to look like a man with a fearfully quick temper.

The clerk prepared to pay the money.   75

'How will you have it?' he said.

'What?'

'How will you have it?'

'Oh' – I caught his meaning and answered without even trying to think – 'in fifties'.   80

He gave me a fifty dollar bill.

'And the six?' he asked dryly.

'In sixes,' I said.

He gave it me and I rushed out.

As the big door swung behind me I caught the echo of a roar of laughter   85
that went up to the ceiling of the bank. Since then I bank no more. I keep my money in cash in my trousers pocket and my savings in silver dollars in a sock.

Stephen Leacock   *My Financial Career*

B

When you start work you'll need a bank account.

Now that you've left school you have a new-found status in the world. So, you'll need a Lloyds Bank Current Account to help manage your money, and open the door to all the other financial services you'll eventually need.

To Lloyds Bank you will be an important individual – a customer. Our staff will make the effort to help you, tell you which of our services will meet your needs. To Lloyds everyone opening an account for the first time is important, because we want to be your bank for many years to come.

"But do I really need a bank account?"

A fair question. For most people their first full-time job is not the first time they have had an income. Holiday jobs, Saturday jobs, paper rounds, pocket money – all these are sources of income that pupils and students will have enjoyed which until now you may have been saving in a Black Horse Young Savers Account. So you'll know the value of money and how to handle it.

A regular income from full time employment is different. Quite simply there is more of it. More to manage. Probably there are more calls on your money as

well. Contributions to the family budget, fares to and from work, lunches at work. Not all the income is available for spending.

The money that is 'yours' to spend will, even so, be more. So your ambitions will grow with it. Albums not singles, more expensive clothes. Holidays with friends, maybe abroad. Some you can pay for out of income, some you will want to save up for.

Possibly you could handle all this new-found wealth using cash. But increasingly it is impractical to do so. For many transactions a cheque is easier and more acceptable. Many employers nowadays pay their employees by cheque or direct to a bank account rather than with cash. For regular payments, standing orders from your account are convenient and time saving. And for saving for a holiday or a car, or whatever, a Lloyds savings account earning interest is a lot better than putting your money in a jam jar.

FREE BANKING
As an incentive to open an account with us, we will run your Current Account free of normal bank charges for the remainder of the year in which you leave school and the following year, providing you keep your account in credit.
The sooner you open your account, the longer it will be run free of charge.

"What facilities do I get as a first time customer?"

A cheque book: you can open a Current Account with as little as £1. If you're starting work then your first pay cheque will be fine.

There are a few very simple formalities, which you can complete at whichever branch of Lloyds is most convenient for you. We will let you have a cheque book shortly after. You can use your cheque book to pay other people rather than use cash, or you can use it to withdraw cash from your account.

Regular statements will help you keep track of your money, what you've spent it on and when.

Paying-in: perhaps, until now, you've been a Black Horse Young Saver in which case you'll know that paying money into an account is easy. Paying money into your Current Account is simple too. You can do it at your own branch with a normal paying-in slip (you're given a book of these when you open an account) or by using a form known as a Bank Giro Credit at any other Lloyds branch or at most other banks.

Ask at your own branch for a pre-addressed Bank Giro paying-in book.

A Cheque Card: if you are in regular employment we will normally issue you with a Cheque Card when we receive your first salary payment. A Cheque Card makes cheques you write up to £50 as good as cash, because Lloyds guarantees payment to anyone who accepts a cheque for up to this amount.

A Cashpoint Card: although cash is used less nowadays it is still an essential part of our modern society. To give our Current Account customers quick and convenient access to their cash, we have installed 1,500 Cashpoint machines in over 1,000 locations, many of which are open outside normal banking hours, 7 days a week. A Cashpoint Card is free to all our customers and you can draw up to £100 a day with it, if your account can stand it.

Preliminary work on A

1 Read the passage again. As you go through it, make a list of any points you don't understand and any questions you would like to ask.
2 Go through the five stages of the reading route on p. 12.
3 Make a list of the main things the writer does. Beside each one write: (a) why he does it and (b) your opinion of his behaviour.
4 Go through the notes you made for (1). Try to work out your own solution to these problems.

Preliminary work on B

Copy and complete the following table:

Item	What it means	How you can get it (+any limitations)
Cheque Card		
Free Banking		
Cashpoint Card		

Questions on A

1   Why did the author ask to see the Manager?
2   What leads the Manager to ask if he is one of Pinkerton's men?
3   Why does the author withdraw all his money as soon as he has deposited it?
4   How does he attempt to cover up his embarrassment?
5   Explain in your own words the meanings of the following words and phrases as they are used in the passage:
      cross the threshold (l. 3)
      self-evident (l. 19)
      vibrating (l. 55)
6   One of the ways in which the writer emphasizes the humour of the situation is by commenting on the way in which people spoke. Quote two examples of this and explain in your own words the exact meaning of each.
7   What impressions do you get of the author as he presents himself? Support your answer by referring to particular details in the passage.

Questions on B

1   Explain in your own words the difference between the following pairs:
    a)   Cheque Card and Cashpoint Card
    b)   Income from full time employment and income you may have had before.
2   How can you qualify to have a Cheque Card?
3   How can you qualify for Free Banking?
4   The leaflet is out to 'sell' the idea of a bank account to people just starting work. What are the main advantages it lists?

Questions on A and B

How have the writers of the Lloyds leaflet tried to overcome the anxieties of people like Stephen Leacock? Do you think they have succeeded?

Directed writing

1   The manager and the accountant in passage A have a conversation about the author, shortly after he has left the bank. Write down what they say to each other.
2   Suppose Stephen Leacock tried to open an account today in Lloyds. How do you think he might get on? Write a story about what you think might happen.

Coffee

There are two main varieties of coffee: Arabicas grow on high, wet, tropical mountain slopes and provide coffee with wonderful flavour and aroma, and a good whack of acidity, without which coffee tastes boring. Robusta coffees grow at lower altitudes, need less rainfall, and crop profusely. They are heftier, with less finesse but great strength and body. Arabicas on their own can be wishy-washy and thin. Almost all blends contain both Arabicas and Robustas, perhaps from six or eight areas or countries.

Most beans (red 'cherries' at this stage) are laboriously picked by hand, hulled, then sorted by size and quality and also to remove the 'stinkers' – beans whose embryos have died within them. A single 'stinker' will pollute a whole bag of beans, making the coffee smell and taste extraordinarily foul. Life must have been very complicated before the electronics revolution. The 'stinkers' look the same as all the others to me, but when subjected to ultra-violet light they glow white like capped teeth or dandruff in a disco. The computerized dalek sorts goodies from baddies.

Coffee is only recognizable as coffee once it has been roasted. A skilled roaster can tell by the smell, the popping sound of cracking beans and the colour when to stop. Every few seconds he scoops a sample from the whirling beans and peers at it. Thirty seconds too long and he'll have burned a batch.

Unroasted coffee beans will stay fresh for years, but once the beans are roasted they quickly lose their quality. The idea is to drink coffee within hours of roasting and grinding but even coffee-buffs will allow three weeks in roasted bean form if the coffee is made as soon as it is ground. Vacuum packing helps, of course, and freezing keeps coffee excellently, even when ground. (You need to thaw it before brewing, however, or you get a pretty chilly cup of coffee.)

Coffee has had a chequered history. The fairy story part is that a third century Arabian goatherd observed his goats behaving mighty merrily after eating the berries, so he ate some too. The local monks, seeing the effect on him, made a brew of the fruit and found it prevented nodding off in church. The habit spread.

Certainly by the fifteenth century Arabia cultivated the bean commercially and protected its monopoly by banning its export other than in ground or boiled form. But pilgrims to Mecca smuggled live beans out anyway and soon the Muslim world, denied alcohol, was living it up in coffee houses all over the Near East. So much so that coffee drinking was frequently banned, both in Muslim and Christian countries. When Pope Clement VIII was petitioned to outlaw the 'hellish black brew' he replied, 'Why this Satan's drink is so delicious it would be a pity to let the infidels have exclusive use of it. We shall cheat Satan by baptizing it'. 40

Coffee proved as unstoppable as booze. Seventeenth-century houses of the City gave birth to the Stock Exchange and to Lloyds. (Stock Exchange servants are called waiters to this day.) But it wasn't until the coffee bar boom of the 1950s and the arrival of instant coffee that the drink really rivalled tea 45 as Britain's national brew. Today we drink two cups of coffee to every two and a half cups of tea. But unlike almost everyone else, the British drink most of it – and presumably prefer it – as 'instant', which is made by brewing coffee, drying the decoction and grinding it to powder.

Prue Leith   *The Guardian* February 2, 1984

Introductory work

1   Divide the passage into two main parts and give each a title.
2   Give each of the paragraphs in each part a title.
3   Make **very brief** notes on each of these topics:
     Arabica   Robusta   'stinkers'   keeping coffee fresh
4   List the main events in the history of coffee, using this date list:
     3rd century: 17th century:
     15th century: 20th century:

Questions

1   Give two reasons why the coffee we buy is nearly always a blend of Arabica and Robusta.
2   How are beans with dead embryos detected and removed?
3   Match up the numbers and the letters:
     1)   unroasted beans   a)   only keep if vacuum packed or frozen
     2)   roast beans   b)   keep for a long time
     3)   ground coffee beans   c)   keep for three weeks
4   Where was coffee discovered and how did it get to the Near East?
5   What is the connexion between coffee and the Stock Exchange?
6   Explain in your own words the main differences between the Arabica and Robusta varieties of coffee. Use between 50 and 75 words.
7   Describe what happens from when the coffee ripens to the production of roast beans. Use between 50 and 75 words.

Directed writing

1   Use the information contained in lines 28–49 as the basis of a paragraph of 100–120 words on the topic 'The History of Coffee'.
2   You have been commissioned to write a companion article to this one on the subject of tea. You plan to visit the Tea Centre as part of your research.
     a)   Make a list of the questions you would want to ask there.
     b)   Write a letter, outlining your plans, to:
          The Director, The Tea Centre, Warwick Street, London EC2 5TY.

Writing home

Mira was born in the eastern part of India, the oldest child of an upper-middle-class family. In 1960, at the age of 20, she enrolled at the University of California to study sociology. Mira received letters from her family in India and wrote letters in reply. A few months after arriving in California, she received this letter from her mother.

10 December 1960

A   My affectionate Miru,

You must have received all my letters by now. We have had only three letters from you in the last month and a half. I know you are busy, but I worry if I do not hear from you. Have you received the parcel I sent by sea-mail? I put some pickles and other 'goodies' together and requested your uncle next door to mail it for me. I did not want to let your baba know about this. You know how much fuss he makes over food parcels. He always gives me big lectures that food in America is a thousand times better and more nutritious. As if that is enough! ... Uma's wedding date is now firmed up and it would be some time in February. Please plan to be here and do not tell your father that I suggested it. Everyone would be very upset if you miss the first wedding of the family. The future groom seems like a good boy and Uma and he met a couple of times when the two families went to the movies together. I think she liked him ... Your Ghosh mashima asked me the other day if I was expecting an American son-in-law. Imagine her guts! I retorted, 'Of course not. Our Miru is as she was before and she would not do such a thing. She went to America to study, not to catch a husband.' ... Have you made some friends? How do you spend your weekends and evenings? Surely, you do not study all the time.

I have to end this letter and get back to the invitation lists. Mejo mashi and I have been digging out all the names of relatives to make a good list and not to leave out anyone. Most of our shopping is complete except the jewellery. We do not want to pick them up until just before the wedding. It's not safe. Oh, Mira, you should have seen the diamond and ruby necklace! It is just beautiful! Write soon and remember the wedding date.

Your mother

B   This is the letter which Mira *wished* she could write her mother in reply:

My dear Ma,

With every letter from you I have an increasing feeling of a distance between us. I cannot explain it even to myself. On the one hand, I know why you are worried about my health, about my life and about my safety. Yet, I thought I had gone ten thousand miles to get away from this protective love which makes me feel suffocated sometimes. It breaks my heart to tell you this and I can never bring myself to say so. What a strange dilemma! I read between the lines of your letters and sometimes I feel like screaming with frustration and anger. What are you fantasizing about my life here? In case I fall in love with an American or whoever, be sure I will do what I wish to do. If you think that you can dictate my life from such a distance, you are under some illusions. But, you know that it's not so easy for me to act the way I would like to. I do not know why. Even when some young men ask me out, your face and the rest (aunts, neighbours, all) appear in front of my eyes. What is this inner restriction? I cannot talk about it to anyone here and I cannot talk about it, least of all, with you. It's not just being free to mix with American men, in different things I feel a tug from behind. I wish I had some power to tear away from this tug and pull ... I also wish I could do everything a good daughter is supposed to do, the way you brought me up. Believe me, it would be so very satisfying to be your good daughter who does not tarnish the name of the family or the wish of her parents, especially her mother. While I am in this interminable conflict, I seem to have no choice but to remain in this tension and confusion. I shall continue to try to please you as much as I can until some part of me gives way. I like my life here and yet I miss India, the family and most of all <u>you</u> so intensely sometimes. Sometimes, I feel I am walking in my sleep and this is a big dream after all. Is it really possible for me to close my eyes and finish my studies and be back exactly the way I came and everything would be just fine for ever. Oh, God, I wish I had some idea how to deal with these problems ... I must sleep; there is a 8.30 class tomorrow. I am so tired.

Your loving and confused daughter

C   This is the letter Mira *really* wrote:

January 1961

Respected Ma,

It was nice to hear from you and get all the news. I am happy to know that Uma's wedding date is firmed. February is a difficult month for me. The classes would be in full session and it would be a loss of nearly three to four weeks of my work here. This break will really be hard for me and I am not so sure I really want to be there only for a wedding between two people who do not even know each other well. No, don't worry. I am not talking about my choosing my own husband or anything like that. But, it seems strange to me when I tell my American friends the way marriages take place in our families. I seem to feel a bit embarrassed about it all. Perhaps, I am not making myself very clear. There are things I feel more and more strange about our customs and it's no point telling you all this. I know you will begin to see mountains out of molehills. Perhaps, baba and I could talk about these things a bit better. At any rate, I shall try.

Thanks so much for sending the food parcel. No, I won't tell baba a word. I am waiting eagerly for it. The pickles! Even the idea makes my mouth water! By the way, please tell Ghosh mashima that Miru has not changed that much yet. And, suppose I do marry an American, is it really the end of the world, ma? I thought you like fair-skinned tall men! (Well, I am joking.) Is Uma really happy about this match? I guess I should not say things like this at this point. Forgive me. This letter has been a bit confused and please don't read between lines, now. I must stop and shall write a longer one perhaps, this weekend. I must rush. *Pranam** to you and baba and greetings to all.

Your Miru

D   A week later:

January 1961

Ma,

This is a quick note to tell you that I am making plans to come in February. If I can finish some of my term-ending papers beforehand I may be able to come without feeling too guilty. It would be wonderful to see you all again. It would be good for me to be back in the family and taste all the good cookings of a wedding. Do you think I should bring a separate gift for Uma from here? Something she might like? Do ask her and let me know. I am terribly busy, but well. I take a glass of milk every night and feel wonderful every morning! The parcel is not here yet.

How are you and baba? I wrote him a long letter giving all details of our university and life here. Has he received it yet? Please take care of yourself and don't go out everyday on errands. How is everyone? My *pranam* and love.

Miru

*Pranam: greetings, best wishes

Karen Payne (editor) *Between Ourselves*

Introductory work

Letter A
1 Make a list of all the people named in the letter.
2 Write brief notes on your first impressions of the mother.

Letter B
3 Write brief notes on the main things that Mira objects to about her Mother's influence.

Letter C
4 Make notes on what Mira says about marriage in this letter.

Letter D
5 List, in note form, the reasons Mira gives to explain why she has changed her mind.

Questions

Letter A
1 If food in America is 'a thousand times better' than in India, why has the mother sent the daughter a food parcel?
2 What reasons does she give for insisting that Mira attends Uma's wedding?
3 How much does she know about her daughter's life in America? What are your reasons for thinking this?
4 What impressions do you get of the mother's attitude to her daughter, and why?

Letter B
5 What does Mira mean by the word 'fantasizing' when she asks 'What are you fantasizing about my life here?'
6 She asks 'What is this inner restriction?' Shortly afterwards she uses a different phrase to express the same idea as 'inner restriction'. Quote the phrase and explain what it means.
7 In about 60 of your own words summarize Mira's attitude towards her mother as expressed in this letter.

Letter C
8 Mira gives two reasons for not going to Uma's wedding. What are they?
9 In what way is Mira's mother likely 'to see mountains out of molehills' or 'read between the lines' of the letter?

Letter D
10 Mira gives three reasons for changing her mind and coming to Uma's wedding. What are they?

All letters
11 What impression do you get of Mira's family's life in India?
12 In what way and for what reasons is Mira experiencing conflict between her upbringing and her new way of life?

Directed writing

1 Write a letter from Mira to an American college friend in which she explains about her family and the tension she is experiencing.
2 a) Write of an occasion in your own life in which you have experienced conflicting loyalties.
or b) Write a short story on the theme of 'divided loyalties'.

3. *Test units*

Touring theatre

The text that follows describes what happens when a touring theatre company visits a theatre to put on a production of *Hamlet* for a week.

No one on the production staff of a touring company ever has a free Sunday. Sunday is the day of the 'get-in' – the theatrical word for moving house. The scenery has to be set on a strange stage, the costumes and wigs set out in strange dressing rooms, the lighting rigged and pre-set – all of which takes the best part of the day, apart from travelling time. 5

The costumes arrive hanging in eight box-shaped wardrobes, gaily painted with stripes or clouds or animals. Inevitably they are never quite ready. The wardrobe mistress and her assistants immediately set about sewing, or dyeing, or repairing them further. Some are being sprayed with aerosols of grey paint to age them. One still has to be made – for the English Ambassador, a role 10 that was cut early in rehearsal and only restored at the last moment. 'I've told them he can't be put back till his frock's ready,' says a harrowed wardrobe mistress. To the wardrobe, all costumes, male as well as female, are 'frocks'.

One of the scenery drapes has been left behind in London by mistake and someone has been told to bring it. The props travel in skips and are being set 15 out in the dressing rooms or on tables behind the stage, one left and one right, according to the entrance at which they will be needed.

Every theatre raises different problems. The New Theatre, Oxford, has what is called a 'bastard prompt corner' – that is, it is stage right instead of the usual stage left. The deputy stage manager, who is going to operate it, 20 has to discover how much, or rather how little, of the action can be seen from there, besides mastering all the switches which confront one like a pilot's panel. While operating the cue lights, the DSM is also following 'the book' – the acting text as finally amended – to prompt any actor who 'dries'. It is early on Monday morning, the day of the technical and dress rehearsals. 25 Most in evidence are four deputy or assistant stage managers – Marje, who will 'run the corner', Garth, who operates the music and sound effects, Ted, who supervises the setting and striking (taking on and off) of stage furniture from scene to scene, and Lance, who is responsible for sending everyone on with the correct props – be it a dagger or crown they should be wearing, a 30 scroll or goblet they should be carrying, or Yorick's skull which must be hidden inside the grave convenient to hand for the gravedigger to unearth. The better the actor, the better he is at remembering his own props – but they must always be checked.

One of the less enviable tasks of the stage management, usually the junior 35 ASM, is to set off the maroons. A maroon, which is the size of a large cotton reel, is really a highly-compressed firework, which has to be set off well away from the stage to provide the effect of cannon. The rules stipulate it must be inside a welded tank. 'Right! Loud Bang! Everybody ready for a loud bang!' People affect nonchalance and go on climbing ladders or hammering nails 40 but the test explosion, when it comes, makes everybody jump.

Meanwhile, on hands and knees, people are marking the positions of the
corners of the throne, the council table, the Queen's bed, Ophelia's tomb,
with pieces of coloured sticky tape – red for this scene, yellow for that, blue
for another. Small as they are, they have to be found in a hurry in the dark   45
or an actor may have his moves and his concentration ruined by finding that
a table or a chair is a couple of feet out of position.

Another stagehand is moving about the stage being 'lit' in the positions
that will be occupied by the actors. Every theatre's lighting board varies and
the touring company brings and rigs extra lamps of its own. The theatres   50
they play provide their own chief electrician, master carpenter, dressers and
housekeeper.

The company manager is responsible for the delicate exercise of allocating
dressing rooms. 'You learn,' says Clare Fox, 'by bitter experience who can't

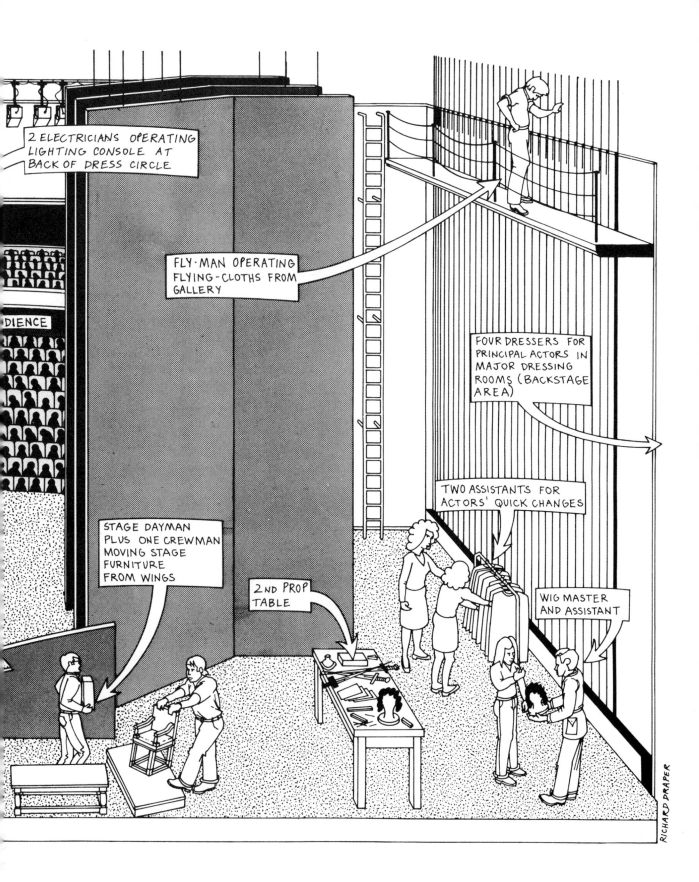

stand whom.' Only the two, or perhaps three or four, principals get a 55
dressing room to themselves. Tradition has it that the more junior the actor,
the farther his dressing room is away from the stage.

The walk-ons, like the wardrobe, are always at the very top of the steep
backstage stairs, which makes little sense in Shakespeare when most of them
are continually changing their costumes and their parts as members of the 60
stage army. In the course of the evening a junior will walk on in perhaps six
different guises as soldier, courtier or servant, with no time to hare up and
down three flights of stairs between each change. Many of them have to use
quick-change areas just behind the wings, dressing directly out of the
travelling wardrobe boxes. 65

Clare describes her role as company manager as a 'glorified nanny – if
anything goes wrong it's my fault'. She it is who finds digs and doctors,
copes with private crises or bad news from home, smooths hurt feelings and,
most important, produces the pay packets every Thursday. They are
ordinary buff pay packets with hard cash inside and the actors' names 70
outside, even those of the stars. Actors on tour need the money in the hand.
Prudently she sees that the money is well concealed about her and handed
over at varying times and places. 'You wouldn't guess I was carrying £8,000,
would you?'

In England the cast are left to find their own accommodation. Many have 75
their favourite places from previous visits, though the reliable old theatrical
digs run by theatrical landladies are disappearing now, because touring is on
so much smaller a scale. 'We've got everything this week from the grandest
hotel to the cheapest digs – no baths after 9.30 p.m. Someone's staying on a
houseboat.' 80

Everyone is required to write his address on the noticeboard inside the
stage door. It is chock-a-block with lists. Call sheets, dressing room details,
good-luck telegrams to the company in general from well-wishers and from
the leading actor, Derek Jacobi, all compete for space and drawing-pins; and
somewhere, hanging on forlornly dog-eared and pin-holed, is the invitation 85
from the local padre representing the Actors' Church Union.

Over in the prompt corner, Marje, the DSM, is sorting out the cue board.
There are rows of button switches operating cue lights – red for 'Stand by',
green for 'Go', some of them irrelevantly labelled 'Orchestra', 'Projector',
'Limes' or 'OP Trap'. These are being altered with sticky tape to 'Musicians' 90
(backstage, not in the pit), 'Maroons', 'Electrics', 'Flies' or 'Houselights'.
Beside the cue board hangs the house telephone by which she can get
through to the front of house, the lighting console, the stage door and so
forth. In front of it is the microphone through which she can address the cast
via the inter-com. 95

Marje is in a bit of a spin because at the last minute the interval has been
moved. All those cues written in the prompt book need altering for several
pages to take account of it. 'And to think I turned down a nice, simple show
because I thought this would be more interesting.'

It is, of course, more interesting. But at a moment like this, with only one 100
rehearsal to finalize everything – they have just decided to combine the
technical and the dress rehearsals for lack of time – the responsibilities for
getting everything right in that prompt corner are fairly frightening.

Questions

1 Use the information in the text and diagram to find out what each of the following people does:

    dresser   stage dayman   fly-man
    wardrobe mistress

2 There are a number of deputy stage managers. What are their jobs?

3 Explain what each of these theatre terms means:

    'get-in' (l. 2)
    'bastard prompt corner' (l.19)
    'the book' (l.24)
    a maroon (l.36)

4 'No one on the production staff of a touring company ever has a free Sunday.' Explain in your own words why not.

5 Why isn't there a public performance on the Monday?

6 How do they ensure that the furniture in each scene is always put in exactly the same place each night?

7 What are the rules governing the allocation of dressing-rooms?

8 How does Marje communicate with
    a)   the musicians
    b)   the cast
    during the play?

9 Explain in about 100 of your own words the job of the Company Manager.

Directed writing

You are a DSM. A young friend has written to you saying that she would like to work in the theatre. She asks you what the work is like. Late on Monday night you write to tell her what you have been doing for the past two days. Write the letter.

A

CYCLING'S BEEN A GOOD IDEA FOR YEARS. SO HAS ALL-BRAN.

More and more people are going for a bike ride as a simple and enjoyable way of helping to keep themselves in shape. We make a breakfast cereal that's also been getting very popular, because it helps to keep your digestive system in shape, simply and enjoyably.

You see, the trouble with a lot of today's foods is that they haven't got enough fibre.

The world's richest source of natural fibre is wheat-bran. And the world's original high-fibre cereal is Kellogg's *All-Bran*. It's made from wheat-bran.

Technically speaking, fibre absorbs and holds water, which speeds up the elimination of waste from our bodies. This helps to prevent constipation and other illnesses caused by too much refined food or lack of exercise. And, according to recent research, an increase in the consumption of fibre may help to prevent more serious diseases, too.

Eat yourself fitter the easy way, like millions of people, with Kellogg's *All-Bran*. It's as natural and enjoyable as learning to ride a bike. And it is becoming just as popular, too.

© 1983 Kellogg Company.

EAT YOURSELF FITTER.

B   Some time ago, sellers of prunes had become exceedingly discouraged in their
efforts to persuade Americans to eat prunes, even in the quantities consumed
in former years. The California Prune Advisory Board turned to a
psychologist, Dr Dichter. The variety of hidden meanings the prune held to
Americans astonished him. The prune's image was riddled with meanings,   5
all unfortunate.

When word-association tests were tried on people, the first thoughts
that came to the surface of their minds, in reference to prunes, were such
thoughts as 'old maid', 'dried up'. In his studies of the place the word 'prune'
had in the English language he came upon such phrases as 'old prune face'   10
and 'dried up old prune'. When his investigators conducted their in-depth
interviews they found that prunes were thought of as a symbol of old age
and lack of vitality. Others remembered that as children they were often
directed to eat prunes because they 'ought to' or because 'prunes are good
for you'. Prunes were associated with boarding-houses where they were   15
served by parsimonious landladies, with stingy, ungiving people, with joyless
puritans. The black murky colour of prunes as commonly served was
commented upon unpleasantly. The colour black was considered somehow
symbolically sinister, and in at least one case the poor prune was associated
with witches.   20

The prune was also thought of primarily as a laxative. In word-association
tests when people were asked to write the first word they thought of in
connexion with prunes, they wrote 'constipation'. Now this laxative image
was not entirely unfortunate. In fact the prune people had once prospered
when the prune's laxative powers first became common knowledge. By the   25
mid-fifties, however, the laxative market was crowded, and the prune's
laxative connotations were felt by Dr Dichter to be a mixed blessing even
though the prune people were still stressing the laxative aspect in their
advertising. Dr Dichter felt this was giving the prune such an unfavourable
image that it was blocking efforts to get the prune widely accepted as a food.   30
'The taste story,' he felt, 'had become lost.' He found that when a grocer
asked a housewife if she wanted prunes she was saying to herself, 'No, I
don't want a laxative'.

All this should indicate the dreadful state the poor prune had got itself
into. What should be done? Dr Dichter felt that what was needed was a top-   35
to-bottom surgery job on the public's image of the prune so that the public
could 'rediscover' it as a brand-new fruit. The whole concept of the prune as
a dried-out fruit for people in need of a laxative was recast into a more
'dynamic' image under his guidance by the California prune people. The aim
in stressing 'the new wonder fruit' was to reassure housewives that it was   40
now perfectly acceptable to serve people prunes. Overnight the prune became
a delightful, sweet fruit, almost a candy, if you were to believe the ads. The
new imagery showed prunes in a setting as far away as you could get from
the dark, murky, old-maidish look of old in which four black prunes were
shown floating in a dark fluid. In the new ads gay, bright colours were used,   45
and childish figures were shown playing. Later the image figures of 'youth'
gradually changed from children to pretty girls figure-skating or playing
tennis. And where prunes were shown they were in bright gay-coloured
dishes or shown against white cottage cheese. With the pictures were jingles

saying 'Put wings on your feet' and 'Get that top of the world feeling'. One   50
ad said, 'Prunes help bring colour to your blood and a glow to your face'.
In its public image the prune had become a true-life Cinderella!

As for the laxative angle it was now mentioned in passing near the bottom
of the message. One ad showing the cute figure skater concluded with these
words: '–, and a gentle aid to regularity. When you feel good, good things   55
happen to you. So start eating prunes today till you have energy to spare'.

Questions on B

1   Why did the California Prune Advisory Board consult Dr Dichter?
2   With what kinds of personality did the researchers find that people associated
    prunes?
3   What did Dr Dichter think was wrong with the old idea of the prune as a
    laxative?
4   In the first part of the fourth paragraph the author describes how Dr Dichter
    changed the prune's 'image'. Quote the sentence which sums up his success
    in doing this.
5   List two ways in which prune advertisements were changed in line with
    Dr Dichter's ideas.
6   Explain in your own words the meanings of the following words and phrases as
    they are used in the passage:
        word-association test (l. 7) in-depth interviews (l. 11)
        parsimonious (l. 16)
        symbolically sinister (l. 19) connotations (1. 27)
7   Paragraphs 2 and 3 detail why prunes had become difficult to sell. In not more
    than 100 of your own words summarize these reasons.
8   Paragraphs 4 and 5 explain how Dr Dichter changed the way in which prunes
    were sold. In not more than 80 of your own words describe what was done.

Questions on A

9   What information is given in the advertisement about the importance of fibre in
    the diet? Summarize it in not more than 35 of your own words.
10 Explain the connexion made in the advertisement between All-Bran and
    cycling.
11 In what ways do the pictures continue the message of the words?

Question on A and B

12 In what ways does the Kellogg's advertisement follow the approach used by
    Dr Dichter for advertising prunes?

Going abroad

A

If you're the one...

Dedicated to the One We Love...
That's right — this brochure's dedicated to you!
The holiday you. The sun-drenched freedom-loving you
that can't wait to strip off the clothes of winter and l-a-z-e
in the warmth.

Your choice of a world of exciting destinations: new
environments in which you can live out your dreams,
make new friends, create a whole new image and
lifestyle. Be who you want to be, do what you want to do!

You're the girl who loves the sun —
an all-or-nothing tan.
You dance the night away till dawn.
You're high fashion — take it to the limit.

You're the guy who lives life to the full.
You've a taste for the action, day or night.
Fun to be with, full of life.

And we're the people with dreams like yours.
We take the very best, leave the others the rest,
and create minute by minute, resort by resort,
the laughs, the style, the fun, the sport,
the unique flavour of a very special world,
bursting with energy, excitement and good times.

And you'll love every minute.
Because WE make holidays the way YOU want them.
And that's why *if you're the one, we're the one for you.*

We're the one for you!

Nº1

B

Ibiza is a world into itself. Like the rest of the Balearics this magical little island is Spanish, but its intriguing Moorish flavour sets it apart. The friendly, easy-going islanders have their own distinct dialect and folklore, and the traditional long black Arab-looking costume is still worn by some women. What's more, when you see the dazzling white flat-roofed houses shimmering under a hot unblinking sun it's easy to imagine you're in North Africa and not a part of Spain.

Ibiza's unique character and laid-back, mañana life-style made it a great favourite with hippies and jet setters, yet for some years it was the Cinderella of the Balearics, overlooked in the initial rush to get at its big sister, Majorca. Times have changed. Nowadays more and more people are coming to this sunbaked island to enjoy its idyllic beaches, clean warm sea and lively nightlife. And for this summer, we're also featuring Formentera. This idyllic tiny neighbour of Ibiza is Spain's very own "desert island" – the perfect spot for escapists.

C

SORRENTO ★★ Campania

Michelin map 988 27 — *Local map p 45* — Pop 16 868

Sorrento stands overlooking the gulf of the same name, a town of beautiful gardens and sunsets, sung by poets and writers. This is where Ulysses resisted the call of the sirens, plugging his crew's ears with wax and making them lash him to the mast of his ship. It is also the birthplace of Tasso (1544), the author of *Jerusalem Delivered (p 100)*.

Luxuriant plantations of orange and lemon trees are the pride of the people of Sorrento.

In season daily boat and hydrofoil services run to Capri from Marina Piccola: p 73.

Villa Comunale. — From a terrace there is a magnificent view★★ of the Bay of Naples: a little to the right Vesuvius is silhouetted against the sky; on the left the island of Procida and Cape Miseno are visible in the distance.

St. Francis' Church (San Francesco) (F). — This Baroque church with a bulbous tower casts its shade over 13C cloisters★ whose capitals support arches pointed in the Moorish style.

Correale Museum★ (Museo di Correale) (M). — Open 9.30 am to 12.30 pm and 4 to 7 pm (3 to 5 pm October to March). Closed Tuesdays, Sunday afternoons, holidays, February and November; 1 500 lire. The museum is housed in an 18C palace. On the ground floor, there is a small archaeological collection. Note also rare editions of the works of Tasso, autographed copies and the poet's death mask. Particularly noteworthy are the museum's collections of 17 and 18C furniture, mostly Neapolitan in style (Room 10, a beautiful ebony writing desk inlaid with ivory depicting Aesop's fables), and of china from Dresden, Vienna and Capodimonte (Naples). Among the paintings you will see a Deposition by A. Vaccaro (Room 8), portraits of the Apostles by Lanfranco (Room 9), and a Madonna by del Sarto (Room 16).

Belvedere (A). — Access, 100 lire for visitors without tickets for the Correale Museum. Beyond the Correale Museum, and a garden planted with orange and lemon trees, you reach a terrace jutting over the sea where you can admire the view★★ of the sea and beautiful sunsets.

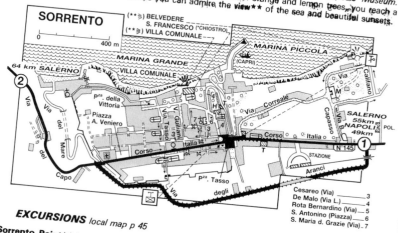

SORRENTO

0 — 400 m

(★★ ≷) BELVEDERE
S. FRANCESCO ("CHIOSTRO")
(★★ ≷) VILLA COMUNALE

64 km SALERNO
② Via del Mare
Via del Capo

MARINA GRANDE

MARINA PICCOLA

(CAPRI)

VILLA COMUNALE

Pza. della Vittoria
Piazza A. Veniero
Via Tasso
Via Giuliani
Via Correale
Corso Italia
Corso Italia

Via Caulino
Via Capasso

SALERNO 55km
NAPOLI 49km
POL.

N 145 ①
STAZIONE
Via degli Aranci

Pza. Tasso

Cesareo (Via) _____ 3
De Malo (Via L.) _____ 4
Rota Bernardino (Via) __ 5
S. Antonino (Piazza) ___ 6
S. Maria d. Grazie (Via) _ 7

EXCURSIONS *local map p 45*

Sorrento Point★★★ (Punta di Sorrento). — 2 km - 1 1/4 miles; plus 1/2 hour on foot Rtn. Go out by ②. At a junction take the Sant'Agata road on the right. Leave the car in the piazza at Capo di Sorrento where the Villa Igea stands and take the road on the right and past the modern church, an alley going down through the gardens and olive groves. From the point you will get a superb view★★★ of the Gulf of Sorrento and the Bay of Naples.

Tour round the Sorrento Peninsula★★★. — 42 km — 26 miles. Leave Sorrento by ② and take the road on the right towards Massalubrense. Past this locality, the road climbs affording splendid views. A picturesque road leads to the pretty beach at Marina del Cantone. At Sant' Agata sui Due Golfi, a delightfully situated resort, take the road to the right, which rejoins the S 145 which you take towards Colli di San Petro. This road along the crests affords many bird's-eye views of the peninsula, the Gulf of Positano and Sorrento. Take road S 163 on the left to Sorrento by way of the picturesque descent to Meta.

D Why?

Technology has made it easy to cross national frontiers physically, but there has been no invention of new mental habits to enable people to cope with foreigners in a new way. For that to happen, the habits of tourists will have to alter. The hidden god of travel is still Karl Baedeker, even though he died in 1859. His guide books have set a permanent pattern, making travel essentially a matter of sightseeing, looking at places rather than at people. His achievement was to find sights that could be guaranteed to be there all the time, to be clearly identifiable, dated and classified according to the amount of admiration they deserved. He made visits to old monuments and to art museums the staple diet of the traveller, drawing attention away from the living inhabitants. To this day, tourism is a course in history, architecture, aesthetics, and the appreciation of hotels and food. The cult of 'sights' has grown so much that most foreign (organized) travel involves virtually no contact with the natives, beyond those who specialize in catering for tourists. The business traveller tends to meet mainly people in his own profession. How different from the itinerary of a modern package holiday is this programme, drawn up by an Englishman, Sir Francis Head, in 1852, before the guide books told tourists what to do. In Paris, he visited the municipal pawnshop, the asylum for blind youths, where Braille, still unknown in England, was being used, a prison, an orphanage for abandoned children, the Salpetrière old people's home, the morgue, the national printing works, the military academy, the national assembly, the public laundry, the dog market in the rue Poliveau and the horses at the Etoile, and finally he attended the lectures at the Conservatory for Arts and Crafts. The rise of bureaucratic officialdom soon stopped that kind of curiosity; but perhaps today a new openness will allow it to express itself again. In former times, the attraction of foreign travel was often that people did abroad what they dared not do at home, which is why foreign countries won reputations for sexual debauchery. (The French considered England as debauched as the English visitors to the Folies Bergères imagined the French to be.) But now that a visit to France is no longer a dangerous adventure, and that an international uniformity exists in so many of the goods and facilities the tourist encounters, where is the excitement, where the new discoveries?

It is to be found in the people. The foreignness in foreign travel today must come mainly from meeting individuals whom one would not normally meet at home.

Theodore Zeldin *The French*

Questions on A

This is the introduction to a travel brochure aimed at a particular group of holidaymakers and offering a particular kind of holiday.

1 What type of holiday resort do you think the brochure is likely to specialize in?
2 What particular group of holidaymakers is it aimed at? What are your reasons for thinking this?
3 The introduction is written in a way that is designed to appeal to the reader. How would you describe the style of the writing? Quote two *short* extracts that illustrate this and explain why you have chosen them.
4 In what ways do the pictures back up the style of the writing?

Questions on B

This is a short extract from the same brochure as A. It describes the attractions of Ibiza and the special entertainments offered in the area by Club 18–30.

5 What are the main features about Ibiza which the brochure considers attractive?
6 What are the main attractions offered by Club 18–30?
7 In what ways does this part of the brochure continue the style and approach of A?

Questions on C

This is an extract from a guide to Italy.

8 What kind of thing does it think visitors to the area will find interesting?
9 In what ways does it contrast with A and B in:
   a) subject matter
   b) style and approach

Questions on D

10 Who was Baedeker and how did he affect modern tourism?
11 The writer says that Baedeker's approach was not the only one in the 19th century. He quotes the case of Sir Francis Head. In what ways did his attitude to tourism differ from that of Baedeker?
12 What was it that put a stop to Head's kind of tourism?
13 The writer says that today tourism is not as exciting as it used to be. Why?
14 What does the writer think is the main point in foreign travel?

Questions on A, B, C, and D

This unit offers three different attitudes to foreign travel: that of the Club 18–30 holidaymaker, that of Baedeker and that of Mr Zeldin.

15 What do you think Zeldin would make of the Club 18–30 brochure? Write a short paragraph commenting on the brochure, as if you were Zeldin.

Directed writing

Write an extract from the Club 18–30 brochure based on the information and illustration in C.

CAR THEFT IS BIG BUSINESS

Over a third of a million vehicles pinched a year – worth over £300 million

Cars worth £85 million never recovered

About 450,000 cars broken into – and valuables worth £50 million stolen

Less than a tenth of this amount recovered

This report takes the car makers to task for giving your car so little protection. And it spells out some things you can do to help make up for the manufacturers' failings

EASY PICKINGS ON THE STREET

Have you ever watched police moving a car that's causing an obstruction? Or asked for help when you've inadvertently locked yourself out of your car? If so, you'll know just how easy it is for someone who knows what to do, and has the right equipment, to get into your car.

As a part of our car tests we check the security of doors, windows, boot or tailgate, bonnet, glovebox, steering column lock, petrol filler lock and sunroof.

Here we tell you what we've found. It adds up to a sorry picture for car owners, and a disgraceful one for car makers. Buying a car is, for many people, the second most costly purchase they make in their life – second only to buying their own home. And yet car makers seem to put car security pretty low on their list of priorities.

We can't publicly blow the whistle on the specific design weaknesses we find in doors and locks, for fear of *worsening* the crime rate. But the makers know the problems as well as we do. They should be making doors more secure, protecting the ignition system and fitting an alarm system as standard (or, at least, offering it as an option). The car makers must take more action to combat the sky-high car crime figures.

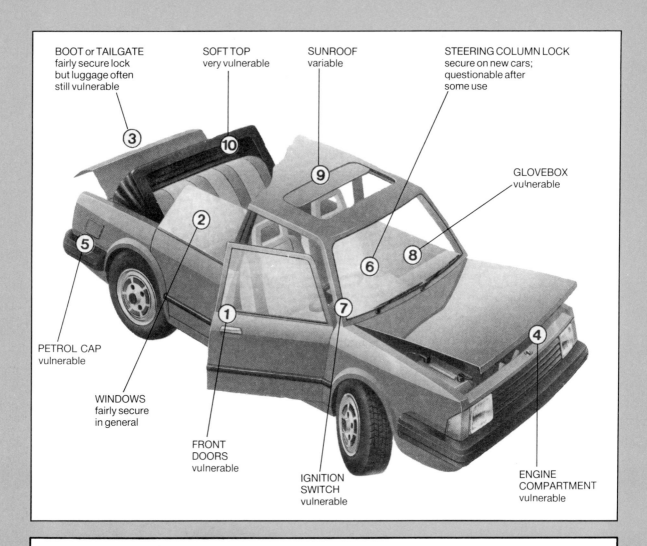

BOOT or TAILGATE
fairly secure lock
but luggage often
still vulnerable
③

SOFT TOP
very vulnerable
⑩

SUNROOF
variable
⑨

STEERING COLUMN LOCK
secure on new cars;
questionable after
some use

GLOVEBOX
vulnerable
⑧

②

⑤

⑥

①

⑦

④

PETROL CAP
vulnerable

WINDOWS
fairly secure
in general

FRONT
DOORS
vulnerable

IGNITION
SWITCH
vulnerable

ENGINE
COMPARTMENT
vulnerable

WHAT YOU CAN DO

There's little you can do to stop an experienced professional car thief. But you can make his life much harder. And you can do a lot to stop the joy rider and the casual, opportunist thief.

▲ **Fit an alarm to your car**
The best alarms will go off *before* a thief actually gets in the car, and they'll also make sure the thief can't start the engine.

▲ **Keep a note of your car's engine and chassis numbers**
They could help you get your car back if it is stolen.

▲ **Always check that all windows are closed, and doors and boot or tailgate are properly locked before you leave your car**
Do this even if you'll be away 'only a few minutes'.

▲ **Make sure your steering column is properly locked**
It engages only at certain angles of the wheel; free movement might make the thief's job easier.

▲ **Never leave valuables in your car**
Why tempt a thief?

▲ **Park off the street**
Your car is safest in a private garage.

ALARMS

How it raises the alarm
The alarms set off either the car's horn or their own sounder—a horn or siren. Using the car's horn might be a bit of a risk if the thief is familiar with the car—he could open the bonnet and cut the horn connexions. A siren is a distinctive sound—people nearby might take notice more quickly. Flashing headlights and indicators, are likely to raise eyebrows, especially at night.

Does it immobilise the car?
Many alarms also knock out the car's ignition. This is obviously a worthwhile protection—if a thief knocks out the horn he may still be unable to drive off.

What triggers the alarm?
Alarms can be triggered by vibration made by a thief before the door is opened, a door being opened, or by something inside (the thief's movement, or the engine being started, for example). The sooner the alarm goes the better.

How persistent is the alarm?
Many of the alarms go off only for a limited time after some sort of disturbance—sensible as it avoids too much unnecessary rumpus. Most importantly, *all* the vibration alarms stopped after a while if accidently triggered off. But a cut-off could be bad if it left the car exposed after the thief's initial attack—some alarms stopped even though the door was still open.

Security against alarm being switched off
The alarm's switch is a weak point. Perhaps the weakest is a key switch outside the car that can be picked easily. Many alarms are worked by a flick switch inside—totally vulnerable once found, though the thief would have to brazen out the noise while looking.

How convenient?
Simple flick switches are quite convenient. A few systems worked with the car's ignition switch—even more convenient.

False alarming?
A car alarm that goes off unnecessarily, because the car is buffeted by gusts of wind, say, can drive people nearby to distraction. Some alarms were more prone to accidental triggering than others.

ALARMS

KEY TO RATINGS: best ◩ ◩ □ ◪ ■ worst

	price	car horn	car indicators	car headlights	its own sounder	ignition	disturbance before car opened	door switches working interior light	extra door, boot, bonnet switches	movement inside car	fixed accessories taken	engine started	how persistent once car attacked	security against being switched off	convenience	preventing false alarm	instructions
A	£21	✓			optional		✓[1]	2		✓	✓		□	□	◪	◩	◪
B	£79				very loud horn	✓	✓	4		✓	✓		□	■	◪	◩	◪
C	£97		✓		loud siren	✓	✓	✓[1]	2	✓		✓	◩	◩	□	□	◪
D	£38		✓		very loud siren	✓	✓	✓	opt	✓			◩	◩	□	□	◩
E	£61	✓			optional	✓				✓			◩	◩	□	◪	◩
F	£35				loud siren	✓	✓	✓[1]	opt	✓		✓	◩	◩	□	◪	◩
G	£53	✓				✓		✓	opt	✓[2]		✓	◩	◩	◩	◪	◩
H	£27				loud siren	✓		✓	2		✓	✓	[6]	◩	◪	◪	■
I	£16	✓		✓				✓	opt	✓			□	◩	□	◪	◩
J	£40	✓		✓		✓		✓	2		✓	✓	□	◩	◩	◪	◩
K	£19	✓			optional	✓	✓	✓	opt				◩	■	◩	[4] ◩	◩
L	£20	✓		✓	optional	✓		✓[1]	2			✓	□	■	◩	◩	◩
M	£46				loud siren	✓		✓[1]	4			✓	□[5]	□	◩	◩	◩
N	£27				feeble siren	✓	opt	✓[1]	opt	opt	✓		□	◩	◩	◩	◩
O	£17	✓		✓		✓	opt	✓	opt	opt			□	◩	◩	■	◩

[1] no alarm if courtesy light bulb has failed
[2] detects air movement in car
[4] but vibration detector can be switched off while leaving other protection active, to avoid false alarm
[5] ◩ if triggered by extra switch
[6] not rated – our samples incorrectly assembled

Questions

1   The writer suggests two ways in which one can find out how easy it is to break into a car. What are they?

2   The article distinguishes between two categories of car thief. Explain this distinction in your own words.

3   Why is it preferable for the alarm system to include its own horn or siren?

4   Why do some alarms switch off after a limited time, and why is this a problem?

5   Explain in your own words what 'False alarming' is and why it is a problem with some alarms.

6   Explain in your own words the meaning of each of the following words and phrases:
> blow the whistle (part A)
> opportunist (part A)
> unnecessary rumpus (part B)
> totally vulnerable (part B)

7   '... the manufacturers' failings...' Read the text on page 77 and then explain in your own words how and why the writer thinks that car manufacturers are failing. Write between 75 and 100 words.

8   Write about 150 words describing and explaining the main weak points in modern cars. Use the diagram on page 78 and these notes as the basis for your writing. The numbers refer to the diagram.
  1)   locks quite efficient – but still easy to get door open
  2)   better than they used to be – but easy to smash
  3)   difficult to beat lock – but problems with: hatchbacks, estate cars, cars with central locking
  4)   easy once you've got the car door open
  5)   locks often rather feeble
  6)   locks get worn – then easy to beat

9   Write about 50 words summarizing the most important points to look for when buying a car alarm.

10   The article in *Which?* from which these extracts come picks a *Best Buy* and lists car alarms that are *Good Value* and *Worth thinking about*. Study the table on page 79 and pick **one** car alarm for each of these three categories. Explain why you chose each one.

Directed writing

Use the material in this unit to help you write an advertisement for a new car alarm, to be printed in a popular newspaper. You should include references to these points: the need for a car alarm – main features – special features – price.

Rubbish!

Recycling waste in the Third World

Sounds of hammering metal fill the air of Pumwani, a down-at-heel suburb of Nairobi. The people are migrants from the Kenya countryside who found little reward in tugging a livelihood from a grudging and arid soil. They came to the city, hoping for work but found little except high food prices and unemployment; certainly few formal jobs.

What could they do? For them there is no dole, no retraining or temporary employment schemes. Instead there is that hammering: informal work, making buckets and oil-lamps and washing bowls and other household hardware out of scrap metal recovered from junked motorcars. Using simple hand-tools and primitive machinery, itself hacked out of steel plate with a hacksaw and a home-made chisel, they carve themselves a livelihood.

The vigour, their crude skills and their determination to make a living are an inspiration from which we in Britain might learn.

I am enthralled by the ingenuity with which the Third World employs its wastes. Collectors in Cairo use the wheels of battle tanks, knocked out in the killing-grounds of Sinai, for their donkey-carts; nothing else is robust enough to withstand the heavy loads and pitted, sand-strewn roads.

I recently followed a Ford V8 'Pilot' along an Andean mountain track. It had been patched so often that little original car was visible. On my return, Ford told me the model had ceased production in 1933; yet it still served, not

as a museum piece but somebody's faithful workhorse, half a century later. Walk through the back streets of Cairo or Calcutta and you can buy any part for any car that ever was, just so long as it has been around long enough to be stolen or crashed. Yet, in Britain, insurance companies refuse to reduce their enormous repair costs by using parts from nearly new crashed hulks that they themselves own.

Third World recycling usually starts at the garbage dump. Manila's huge landfill at Tondo receives garbage from nearly two million people every day and has existed so long it is now one of the highest points in the city. As each truck tips its load it is surrounded by a hoard of men, women and, horrifyingly, children of all ages, who use steel hooks to grab any object that may have a small resale value: bottles, cartons, metal, rags, broken plastic buckets and even used torch batteries for the miniscule quantities of brass and zinc they contain.

Another type of scavenger precedes the garbage truck, often with a small cart on rattly wheels, picking up anything saleable that the householder has stacked on the pavement. In Mexico, they are contemptuously referred to as *moscas* (flies) by those lucky enough to have a pleasanter occupation.

Although the employment may be informal and the working conditions often appalling, the scavenging system is by no means lacking in organization. Take, for example, glass recycling in the Philippines. It is like a river. Each household is a spring from which used bottles arise. The scavengers form the multitude of tiny streams that trickle into the junkshops: small, family-owned warehouses scattered around residential areas.

The junkshops own pushcarts which they lend out to the scavengers, who collect a mixed load from which the junkshop owner separates the saleable bottles (for sale to makers of fish sauce and soft drinks), and broken ones which are sold to a dealer. The dealers form the big rivers through which flow thousands of tonnes of broken glass every year. The rivers feed the ocean of white-hot molten glass in the furnaces of San Miguel brewery, which supplies beer to 50 million people, and the whole cycle begins again.

On an assignment for OXFAM, I helped small plastics recycling enterprises in one of the poorest parts of Cairo. They reduce plastic scrap into small chips, the size of cornflakes, and feed them into tiny moulding machines: partly hand-operated and quite unlike the electronically-controlled robots in modern plastics factories. Salah Mahmoud Mohammed, whose chickens live alongside, moulds a range of small products, of low quality and price, like toy spectacles, for children to wear in mocking imitation of their elders, with lenses in virulent crimson polystyrene, and snap-on earpieces in a sickly shade of green polythene.

Thousands of tiny workshops like Mahmoud's make an important contribution to the nation's economy. Is there any limit to how many jobs can be created, how much raw materials or energy saved by recycling? Dr Mounir Neamatalla, a Cairo management consultant, gave me an explanation that must astonish those of us who lament the wastefulness of our over-packaged society: 'Unfortunately, there is not enough waste to support the demand for low-cost products from recycled materials'.

Jon Vogler   *The Listener* July 12, 1984 (adapted)

B **Waste factsheet**

All information adapted
from **Norman Myers** (editor)
*The Gaia Atlas of
Planet Management*

Figure 1   Recycling

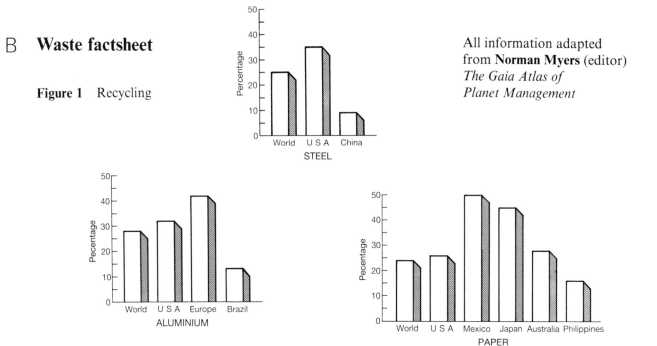

Figure 2   How Western Industrialized Countries could increase recycling

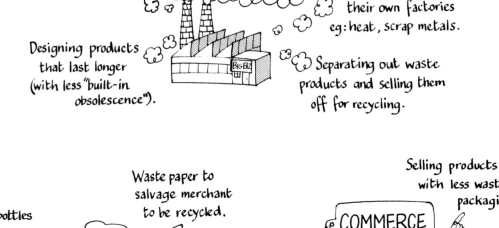

Figure 3
Waste per person
per day

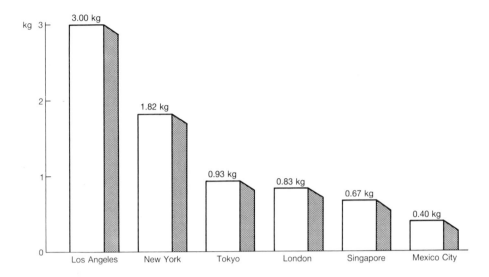

Questions on A

1. What reason does the writer give to explain why the people have moved from the countryside into Nairobi?
2. Where do they find the materials to make household hardware?
3. Explain in your own words why the writer admires them.
4. Why does he say that tank wheels are suitable for Cairo donkey-carts?
5. Why does the writer take British insurance companies to task?
6. What is the difference between the scavengers described in paragraph 6 and the *moscas* described in the next paragraph?
7. The description of glass recycling in the Philippines compares the process to a river. Explain the comparison in about 60 of your own words.
8. Why was the writer in Cairo?
9. What limits the activities of those involved in plastics recycling in Cairo?
10. The writer is clearly very much in favour of recycling in the Third World. What reasons does he give for his attitude? Summarize them in about 200 of your own words.

Questions on B

1. Study Figure 1 and explain in not more than 50 of your own words what the rest of the world could learn from Europe, Mexico and Japan about recycling.
2. Using information from Figure 2 explain how raw materials could be saved in the area of the packaging of goods.
3. Figure 3 shows a contrast between the situation in the USA and elsewhere in the world. Explain the contrast in one sentence.

Directed writing

1. In what ways could the western world learn from the developing world about recycling? Write a short article (100–150 words) expressing your views.
2. In what ways could the salvaging and recycling of waste be
   a) encouraged;
   b) made easier?
   Write between 100 and 200 words explaining what you think.

The police

A

When villains start working 9 to 5, so will we.

Like most other white collar workers, police officers work at least eight hours a day, five days a week.

There the similarity ends.

In a place like London, accidents, football matches, demonstrations, crime, tourists, and the like keep us busy twenty four hours a day, seven days a week.

 HARROW: An old lady hasn't been seen for a few days, and the milk is piling up on her doorstep. A Woman Police Constable breaks in and finds her dead on the floor. Foul play? The Inspector and Police Surgeon are called in.

And since quite a lot of our work involves dealing with London's anti-social elements, anti-social hours are what we tend to work.

You could find yourself up well before the lark on Early Turn, 6 am to 2 pm.

Or you could be putting in a hard day's night while most law-abiding folk are comfortably parked in front of the television.

 BERMONDSEY: The Community Liaison Officer visits a local youth club to talk about the dangers of drugs and glue sniffing. The kids complain about being 'picked on', so the message doesn't get through this time.

Look on the bright side, though.

While everyone else is slaving away at work, you can spend an afternoon in the garden or at the squash club.

So much for routine.

There's not much chance of anyone settling into a comfortable routine in the Metropolitan Police.

 **COVENT GARDEN:** A man is seen trying to feed an American Express card into an all night cash dispenser. It turns out he is high on LSD and the card is high on our stolen list. That won't do nicely at all, sir.

It's one of the few occupations where you can turn up for work and not have an inkling of what the day holds in store for you. You could be called to the scene of a fatal accident, or an armed robbery.

Or you could spend the afternoon in a community centre helping to sort out old people's problems.

Every day, you'll find yourself in situations that demand something different from you.

 **ISLINGTON:** A man tries to pass a stolen cheque in an off licence. The manager calls us. The man runs off. A woman police officer stops him and finds he's carrying several stolen credit cards.

By turns, you'll be a tourist guide, marriage guidance counsellor, diplomat, child psychologist, criminologist, social worker, self defence expert, first aid specialist, lawyer and speaking clock.

 **CROYDON:** The Area Car stops a red Jaguar XJL2 that's being driven erratically. A computer check on the car reveals it's stolen. A computer check on the driver reveals he's wanted in connection with a number of burglaries.

Every one of these jobs requires different individual qualities.

You'll need all of them to get you into the Metropolitan Police Force.

How do you measure up?

First of all, you must be at least 168 cms tall if you're a woman and at least 172 cms if you're a man.

 FULHAM: A bomb reported in a shop doorway. Chief Inspector and C13, Anti Terrorist Branch called out to assess the situation. The Explosives Officer confirms our worst suspicions were unfounded. Better safe than sorry.

Ideally, the academic qualifications we're looking for are around five good 'O' levels.

Nevertheless, people who've got a string of 'A' levels won't get in if they don't possess all the right personal qualities.

You'll need a lot of common sense, a genuine concern for people, a strong sense of fair play, an agile mind in a fit body and a well developed sense of humour.

 SOHO: Two officers spot a man climbing the scaffolding outside an office block. He claims he's looking for his football. They offer to help him look and find all the signs of a break in. The phantom footballer gets booked.

And as these aren't the sort of things we can discern from an application form, you'll have to go through our two-day selection process.

A copper earns every penny.

The pay is very good. Considering some of the things we'll ask you to do for it, it has to be.

 CLAPHAM: An officer in a Panda Car spots a suspiciously parked van. He investigates and finds three men doing a clothes shop. He gives chase and with assistance nabs two of them. A good night's work.

At 18½ (our minimum age), the least you'll start on is £8,520, including London allowances.

If you're a bit more mature, you'll be better equipped to help us. So over 22's start on more.

As you gain experience and make progress in the Force, your salary will keep pace. Although you can be sure the hours won't get any easier.

For further information, phone (01) 725 4575. Write to the Appointments Officer, Careers Information Centre, Dept. MD962, New Scotland Yard, London SW1H 0BG.

These incidents are based on real events, but for legal reasons, the locations have been changed.

What do the police do all day?

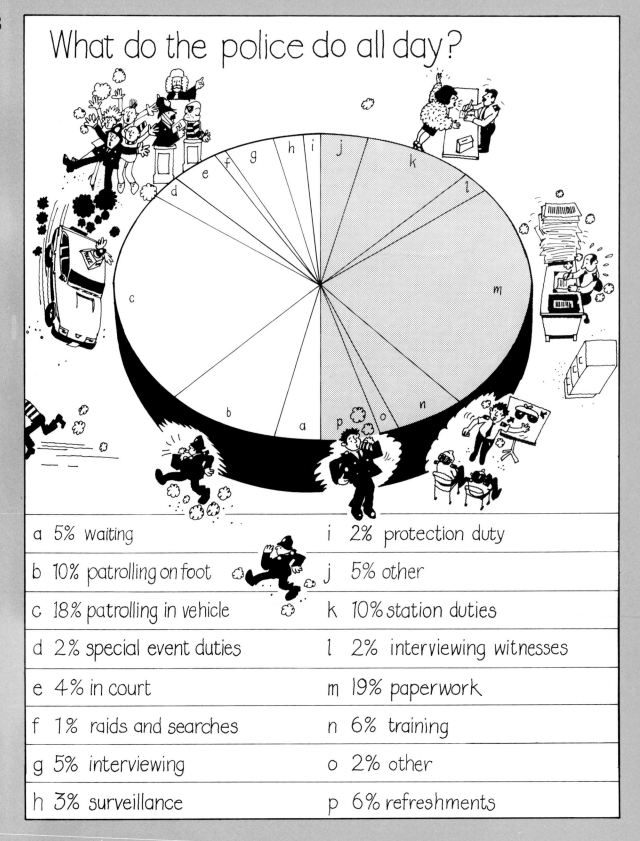

a	5% waiting	i	2% protection duty
b	10% patrolling on foot	j	5% other
c	18% patrolling in vehicle	k	10% station duties
d	2% special event duties	l	2% interviewing witnesses
e	4% in court	m	19% paperwork
f	1% raids and searches	n	6% training
g	5% interviewing	o	2% other
h	3% surveillance	p	6% refreshments

C The British police

The British police are the best in the world – or so the saying runs. This may still be true. But in the past few years the police and their actions have become increasingly controversial. Urban riots, sieges, gun battles, terrorism, corruption and arguments over police powers have ensured that the cosy old image of *Dixon of Dock Green* has gone for ever. Some people have even concluded that Britain has become a police state.

The main worry among the critics of the police over the past few years has been that tendencies towards centralization, high technology, violence and surveillance are combining to place them beyond control by democratic processes. Far from being the servants of the public, the police, the critics say, are becoming autonomous from the rest of society.

To their credit, the police have responded to these criticisms, though in a contradictory way. Some have said that these developments are more or less inevitable responses to rising crime, to increased disorder and to more sophisticated challenges to outdated policing methods. This approach has been dubbed the *fire brigade* style of policing, in which the car, the radio and the computer dominate, and in which police officers are basically responders to reported incidents.

Other elements in the police have tried to revive what is commonly seen as a more traditional approach. Here the aim is on prevention rather than response, on greater personal contact between locally based police and their neighbourhood, and on co-ordination of police aims with those of social workers and teachers. This approach is dubbed *community policing*.

In reality, most policing in Britain draws on a combination of both approaches. At present, the initiative is with the advocates of community policing. The emphasis now is on good police-community relations and good police training. But here, even the most enlightened police planner faces a big problem – police culture.

During the past 20 years, the social status of the police has changed. Repeated calls for better 'law and order' have led to huge increases in police wages. The recruitment of graduates has blossomed. Large injections of capital investment have been put into new technology. As police work has shifted away from the streets and to the desk and the visual display unit, so police social expectations have risen and an ethos of 'professionalization' has emerged. Police have become more middle-class, and indeed earn more than many middle-class occupations such as teachers. In urban areas, many police can now afford to live in pleasant suburbs, commuting into the inner cities where they work. Just as crime has become more white collar, so have the police.

Nevertheless, the overriding image of the police is still that of the crime-fighter. For more than a century, fictional works and television series have depicted policework as exciting, active, physical and dangerous. The aims of policing are clear cut – suppressing crime and trying to pin down criminals. This mythology still dominates police culture and public expectations of the police. It is vigorously sustained by the public, the media and the police alike.

The public, it is argued, needs the myth to sustain the confidence that, when you are in trouble, the police will bring swift and effective aid. The media feeds the myth through its depiction of fictional police work and its reporting of actual police work. In both cases the treatment is highly selective, concentrating on certain crimes (murder, rape, armed robbery, mugging) while largely ignoring others (frauds, traffic offences, theft and most burglaries). And only the most dramatic examples of even selected types of crime are normally depicted, thus painting an extremely misleading and fear-inducing picture of crime. The police themselves help to sustain the mythology. Studies have shown that police highlight the violent, exciting and competitive nature of their work. Police look upon making arrests – 'feeling collars' – as the best test of achievement. Other aspects of police work, which in fact make up the bulk of the job, are seen, at best, as marginal to and, at worst, as getting in the way of 'real policing'.

New Society May 5, 1984

Questions on A

1 Describe briefly the main things you can see in the photograph at the head of the advertisement. What impression does it give of police work?
2 The advertisement contains a simple 'timetable' of events on a typical night. It contains eight items. For each of these make up a short, two or three, title summing up its main features.
3 What is meant by 'anti-social' hours? Why do the police have to work anti-social hours?
4 Does the advertisement suggest any advantages for the individual police-officer in working such anti-social hours? If so, what?
5 The advertisement stresses that police work is very varied. Quote three examples of tasks a police-officer may have to do which illustrate that variety.
6 The second part of the advertisement concentrates on what the police are looking for in new recruits. Explain in your own words what it says about exam qualifications.
7 It lays great stress on personal qualities. Explain in your own words what it means when it says that a police-officer needs 'an agile mind in a fit body'.
8 The advertisement uses a number of words which have a special meaning for the police. Explain what each of these means:
    villains
    anti-social elements
    foul play

Questions on B

1 What percentage of his/her working time does a police-officer spend inside the police station?
2 What activity takes up most of his/her time in the station?
3 What percentage of his/her time does he/she spend out of the station?
4 What activity takes up most of his/her time out of the station?
5 Which combination of activities takes up more of the police-officer's time:
    (a) patrolling by car and on foot, or (b) paperwork and station duties?

Questions on C

1 The first paragraph suggests some events which may have caused people to revise their traditional view of the British police force. Name two of them.

2 In the second paragraph the writer outlines the worries that some critics of the police have. Explain briefly in your own words what these amount to.

3 What is *fire brigade* policing?

4 What is *community* policing?

5 Paragraph 6 explains the way in which police **work** has changed. What are the main features of this?

6 In what ways has the **social status** of the police changed in the same period?

7 The last two paragraphs argue that public, media and the police themselves still agree on an 'overriding image' of the police. Write a sentence summarizing that image.

8 **Why** do the public want to maintain that image of the police?

9 **How** do the media help to create and maintain it?

10 **What evidence** is given that the police themselves like to maintain this image of their work?

Questions on A, B, and C

1 In what ways does B support the arguments put forward in C?

2 C suggests that one idea of police work is that it is *fire brigade* policing. Find examples of this idea in A.

3 C also suggests that other people believe in *community policing*. Find examples of this in A.

4 C argues that the police put forward an image of themselves which is a 'myth'.
   a)   In which paragraphs is this argument presented?
   b)   Are there any elements in A which support this idea? If so, what are they?
   c)   Are there any elements in A which contradict it? If so, what are they?

Directed writing

1 Which picture of the police do you find more satisfactory: that presented by A, or that offered by B and C? Write explaining your opinion and giving your reasons.

2 Suppose the author of A met the author of C as part of a radio or TV investigation into the police: how do you think the conversation might go? Write a script of what they say to each other.

3 Using the material in A, B, and C, and ideas and information of your own, write a balanced view of 'The job of a police-officer'.

Olympic darts

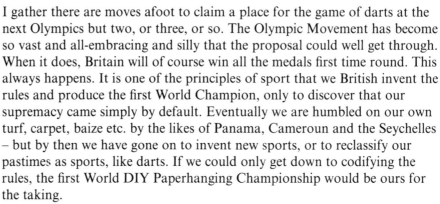

I gather there are moves afoot to claim a place for the game of darts at the next Olympics but two, or three, or so. The Olympic Movement has become so vast and all-embracing and silly that the proposal could well get through. When it does, Britain will of course win all the medals first time round. This always happens. It is one of the principles of sport that we British invent the rules and produce the first World Champion, only to discover that our supremacy came simply by default. Eventually we are humbled on our own turf, carpet, baize etc. by the likes of Panama, Cameroun and the Seychelles – but by then we have gone on to invent new sports, or to reclassify our pastimes as sports, like darts. If we could only get down to codifying the rules, the first World DIY Paperhanging Championship would be ours for the taking.

It is hard to make a very logical case, as a matter of fact, against the notion of Olympic darts. People are already winning medals for firing off bullets and arrows at targets; and since darts makes no use of missile-firing machinery, it is actually a truer test of basic human coordination than these accepted events. It is true that not many countries have shown an interest in darts so far, but most show an interest in beer, which is a start. The Americans are catching on, and the Russians will surely be keener still, once they realize that their stock of big fat men is incomparably larger than ours.

The only real problem that confronts the Olympic Committee – if the original atmosphere of darts is to be maintained pro tem – is the invention of an electronic referee with multi-lingual facility, capable of yelling 'Cent quatre-VINGTS!' or 'Hundert ACHTZIG!' or their equivalents, at the appropriate moment. Those polite instructions the players receive as they get near a finish ('Basil, you require sixty-nine') should probably be done in French. 'Basile, vous desirez soixante-neuf' is so much more refereed.

Now you may say that the game of darts is set too deep – unfairly deep – within our own social patterns. But to make that stick, you will have to explain why leaping about in a leotard trailing a length of ribbon (alias 'Tumbling' I believe) should be considered an Olympic sport either. The only people interested enough in this to be good at it appear to be the Russians, for whom this activity evidently satisfies the same psychological need – for a kind of one-man militarism – as baton-twirling does for the Americans.

Besides, anyone can tell, looking at a dart board, how well the contestant has done. To know how well a tumbler has curlicued her ribbon is not possible. It is a matter of opinion. Worse, it is a matter of taste. And the Russians themselves necessarily create the taste by which their prize-winning ribbon-flinging is judged. The British, to a lesser but still significant degree, have for some time dictated what a good ice-dance consists of, to the equal and opposite discomfiture of the Russians. Thus the pseudo-aesthetic aspect of sport goes pirouetting out of control.

In diving the degree-of-difficulty 'tariffs' mean that the debatability of the whole exercise is magnified by multiplication. The ski-jumper who leaps 110 metres while inelegantly flailing his fins (all ski-jumpers are momentarily transmogrified into penguins) is beaten to the gold medal by the poncy perfectionist who does 102 metres while standing rigidly to attention –

usually much to the disgust of the crowd, who recognize that it's a hopeless mix-up of quantity and quality.

While we're at it, let's admit that even the ordinarily quantitive Olympic events are no longer uniformly credible. The steady upward progress of the pole-vault record, for example, is surely a matter of pole technology. We are getting to the stage where poles bend like hairpins, then snap upright again to send their custodian, *sployng*, over the bar. Within our own lifetime, we can expect to see pole-vaulters disqualified on the grounds that they landed on the outside of the stadium.

All of this can only help the dartists' case. Admittedly these men are, perhaps, over-aggressively unaesthetic. That is, many of them look horrible. But then so do the superheavy weightlifters. The drug-testing rules might be a problem – I imagine competitors are not permitted to harbour equal quantities of blood and lager in their bodies – but otherwise I see no impediment.

Let's go further, and turn the whole occasion into the circus it so obviously wants to be. What price medals for the coconut-shy? Poker? Sheep-shearing? Poohsticks?

Russell Davies *Observer Magazine* February 19, 1984

Questions

1   'This always happens.' (l. 4–5) Explain in one or two of your own sentences what the writer thinks 'always happens'.
2   What reason is given in lines 13–18 for including darts in the Olympic Games?
3   What does he say tumbling and ice-dancing have in common?
4   He argues that ski-jumping competitions are a 'hopeless mix-up of quantity and quality'. (l. 48–9) Explain in your own words what he means.
5   The writer lists two possible objections to the adoption of darts as an Olympic competition. What are they?
6   Explain in your own words the meaning of each of the following **as it is used in the passage**:   codifying (l. 10)   curlicued (l. 36)
                    multi-lingual (l. 23)   momentarily transmogrified (l. 45)
7   Explain clearly and fully the meaning of:
    a)   '. . . the game of darts is set too deep – unfairly deep – within our own social patterns.' (l. 28–9)
    b)   '. . . even the ordinarily quantitative Olympic events are no longer uniformly credible.' (l. 50–1)
8   Explain in your own words the writer's objections to each of the following Olympic events:
    a)   tumbling
    b)   diving
    c)   pole-vaulting
9   Write a paragraph of 120–180 words describing the writer's attitude to the Olympic Games. State your reasons for the points you make.

Directed writing

Imagine that you are a member of the Olympic Committee. You have received a formal proposal that darts should be included in the next Games. Write a press handout (of about 150 words) stating this and explaining the committee's response.

Section C: Literary texts

1. Introductory units

2. Transitional units

3. Test units

1. *Introductory units*

The incline

The quarry was high on the hillside above the little town. The sun was up on the left, and it pierced among the houses with light and shade, so that each house and roof edge looked as if it might cut. Smoke rose from the houses and lay over them as if they were some metal object newly cast and laid in the valley, in the cloudy vapour of its own creation. 5

The slope of the hillside shut away the noise of the quarry. The noise of the town began to come to him instead, and the sound of the local insects, the sound of the shadowy dew splashing from disturbed grass on to his bright boots. He looked at his track behind him, darkening the grass.

The lane turned a corner and went straight down a rocky section. Here 10 there was no sound from quarry or village. Only the bees and flies in the white roses and buttercups, elder and broom, trafficked noisily. The small coppery butterflies flashed in the sun; they lived here in clouds, like midges. Among the rocks that made the floor of the lane just here ran the channels of a beck; the water flashed up the blue glare of steel from ripple and rapid. 15

A wide field away to the right was the railway that mounted the hill from the dock in the town to the quarry. It was a slope laid on the irregularity of

the hill, in some places dug into it, in some places banked above it. Down it would go a railway wagon full of stone, and up at the same time would come an empty truck. A wire cable joined the trucks, and ran up into the quarry buildings and over a great wheel and braked rims. The track was called the Incline. Now on it there was rising a wagon with one squeaking wheel. The descending wagon was out of sight in a cutting, but the empty one moved magically alone, with nothing apparently working on it, up the slope. Then it stopped for a moment while the brakeman at the top made some adjustments to the points away down at the bottom of the Incline, and the pulling wire quivered, and Mason saw it.

The truck sat there without moving. Someone shouted up from the bottom, and someone shouted from the top. The truck moved again and its wheel continued to squeal.

Beyond the Incline there was a wild, wooded, unused field. At the top of it the quarry tips reared up with great ends sloping a hundred feet to a skyline. Stone tipped there rumbled in long avalanches and slides, unsettled for days or months, unbound, dangerous.

William Mayne   *The Incline*

Introductory work

1 Read the passage carefully. Draw a map of the area it describes.
2 Draw a diagram to show how the trucks worked on the Incline.

Questions

1 What does the author mean when he says that 'each house and roof edge looked as if it might cut'? (l. 2–3)
2 What time of day is it?
3 What time of year is it and how do you know?
4 Why did his track behind him 'darken the grass'? (l. 9)
5 What does it mean when it says that the bees and the flies 'trafficked noisily'? (l. 12)
6 The railway incline is described as 'a slope laid on the irregularity of the hill' (l. 17–18). What does this mean?
7 Explain in your own words how the trucks worked on the Incline.
8 Who caused the truck to stop and why?
9 What was the meaning of the two shouts?
10 In the last sentence the stone is described as 'dangerous'. Why?

Directed writing

Write a short story, titled 'The accident' set in the area described in this text.

Sumitra's story

This passage comes from a story about what happens to a family of Ugandan Asians driven out of Africa by the political situation. They settle in Britain.

Before the end of the summer there were more incidents of racial unrest.

A gang of English youths had attacked some Asian boys. The Asian community of Southall suggested forming a vigilante committee. This was frowned on by those who thought that the police were the right people to deal with incidents of this nature. Every night there were discussions at home as they ate their evening meal. Bap felt that the police were not doing enough; Mai was frightened and would not go out alone. Ela and Bimla stood close together at the bus-stop in the evenings. Sandya and Sumitra were anxious and perturbed.

Sumitra had never told anyone about the dream. In the dream she was waiting at the bus-stop one night after work and the thugs had come upon her from behind. 'Paki, Paki!' they screeched as two of them held her arms while the third punched her over and over until her teeth had gone, her eyes were blinded with blood and her ribs kicked and broken. The brave and goodly citizens of Highgate trod over her until, at last, one of them stopped and picked her up. The face of the Good Samaritan was black. Just before she died, she recognized who it was. It was Yusuf, the houseboy (their servant in Uganda).

Sumitra and Sandya started to listen to the phone-in programmes. The race issue was discussed almost every evening for several months. The callers seemed to fall into certain categories. There were the Some-of-my-best-friends type of calls, which went: 'Some of my best friends are black: I don't want you to think I'm prejudiced, but the other day I saw a West Indian woman push a white lady out of the way at the bus-stop'. There were the They've-taken-our-jobs brigade: 'They come over here, black, brown, yellow, take our jobs and our houses, fill the streets with the smell of their cooking . . .'. Then there was the Live-and-let-live party: 'I don't mind immigrants, Nigel. I think it makes life more interesting'. There was also the occasional immigrant complaining of discrimination, or, more rarely, stating that no hostility existed.

The presenters were more uniform. Sumitra noticed that a person calling from the National Front was either cut off immediately or allowed three seconds in which to express a view. She made Sandya stand, watch at the ready, timing each call. The phone-in announcers presented the white liberal attitude, usually recommending unlimited immigration and scolding callers who did not agree for being prejudiced. 'They don't seem to know there's a race problem in this country,' Sumitra said. 'They seem to think everything's great, that everybody loves their neighbours.' Sandya sighed. 'Hmm. I wonder where they live, these announcers, or what schools their kids go to? I wonder if they really ever talk to anyone – I mean really hear what other people are saying?'

'Sometimes,' confided Sumitra, 'I imagine that they don't really exist. They may just be great big mouths, robots, without any ears to hear with – monsters, who can only talk.'

It seemed to be true. The presenters hissed and snapped at anyone who did 45
not say what they wanted to hear, cutting callers off and then adding a
sarcastic comment from within their sound-proofed safety. Freedom of
speech, thought Sumitra, should be two-way. It could be dangerous to deny
people with genuine grievances access to what they felt was the only channel
where they could publicly state their beliefs. 50

Sumitra and Sandya listened to these conversations with amusement and
horror. 'Do you think there should be unlimited immigration?' asked
Sandya.

'I don't think so,' Sumitra told her. 'Britain's a small country, it's hard
enough for those of us here to integrate, let alone allowing more and more 55
people to come in. If we were adapting better it probably wouldn't matter,
but we aren't really accepted as a group, and goodness knows we see enough
of Mai's generation who don't even *want* to be accepted!'

Rukshana Smith *Sumitra's Story*

Introductory work

1 Make a list of the people named in the passage.
2 Against each name make a note of any information you can find about that
   person.
3 Sumitra criticizes the presenters of phone-in programmes because they favour
   only one point of view.
   Work out for yourself
   a) what that point of view is;
   b) how this is done.

Questions

1 Explain in your own words what some people wanted to do after the
   attack by the English youths.
2 Why did other people disagree?
3 Where did Sumitra work?
4 Why does she compare her dream with the story of the Good Samaritan?
5 Paragraph 4 lists three different types of caller to the phone-in programmes.
   Describe them in your own words.
6 What is the 'liberal attitude'? (l. 35)
7 What methods did the presenters use to make sure that the liberal attitude
   prevailed in the programmes?
8 Why did Sumitra think this was dangerous?
9 In the last paragraph Sumitra lists some of the problems involved in integration.
   Explain these in not more than 60 of your own words.
10 What impression do you get of Sumitra and her thinking about the problems
   she and her family are facing?

Directed writing

Suppose Sumitra decided to telephone one of these phone-in programmes. She gets
through to the presenter and tries to explain what she thinks. Write the conversation
they have.

Safe and soundproof

There she sat, pretty as a bumble-bee with her gold eyes and brown hair, attracting even more attention than men with hydraulic grabs on building sites. She sat behind a sheet of plate glass in Dowbridge's window, at a desk that was all made of glass, and she had a mighty mirror behind her.

At her side was a dear little electric furnace, all in white, and on the desk was a guillotine. With this she was demolishing stacks and stacks of documents, cutting them into slivers like bacon, and then turning them round and repeating the process crossways until she had a mound of confetti. When it was knee-high she slid the whole heap into a plastic basket and shot it into the furnace.

Pile after pile of paper the furnace wolfed down with the barest flicker of acknowledgement, and Roger Mauleverer, watching through the window, thought of pine forests in Sweden and Canada, vast stretches of spruce and redwood towering majestically in snow and sunshine, all destined to total extinction after this girl had done with them. He felt quite cross about it, for he liked trees. But he had to admit that the girl was very attractive.

Over her head, right across the plate glass, he could read the inscription:

> CONFIDENTIAL RECORDS EFFECTIVELY
> DESTROYED UNDER GUARANTEE

For the first two weeks that Ghita Waring sat in the window, her boss, who had a flair for publicity, tied a bandage over her eyes so that it was plain she couldn't read the documents she was chopping. But she cut her finger three times.

The following week he put her in dark glasses, but he had to admit that the gold eyes were a loss. So the fourth week he contented himself with a notice on the front of her desk:

> SHE ONLY READS MUSIC
> YOUR SECRETS ARE SAFE WITH HER

Ghita's old headmistress, who happened to pass by and see this, was very annoyed about it and complained that it was a poor advertisement for her

school, but Ghita merely laughed and said she didn't mind; anyway, it was almost true. Though she added that she could read cookery books if the words weren't too long. She managed to conceal her really dangerous gift; if it had been discovered she would hardly have landed the job.

It was a never-failing pleasure for passers-by to stop and watch her, and wonder what she was cutting up now. 35

'That's a will,' muttered Sidey Curtiss to Bill Brewer. 'Bang goes the long-lost blooming heir. Now what's she got?'

'Might be an agreement. See the red seal?'

'There goes a confidential file; some bloke's past history smoking up the chimbley. Pity she couldn't chop up your record, Bill, eh? Just phone police headquarters and tell 'em to send it along in a plain van.' 40

Bill took this bit of humour coldly. 'Why not ask 'er to chop off your fingerprints while she's at it?'

Joan Aiken   'Safe and Soundproof' in *A Bundle of Nerves*

Introductory work

This is the beginning of a short story. Work out the answers to these questions:

Where is it happening?
What is happening?
Who is/are the main character/s?
Why is it all happening?
What will happen next?

Questions

1   Where is the girl sitting?
2   What is she doing?
3   Why is she doing it?
4   Why does Roger Mauleverer think of 'pine forests … destined to total extinction'? (l. 13–15)
5   Why should anyone want a guarantee that confidential records had been destroyed?
6   Why did the boss blindfold Ghita?
7   What other tricks did he think up to achieve the same thing?
8   What does Sidey Curtiss hint about Bill Brewer?
9   What is the meaning of Bill Brewer's reply?
10   Ghita 'managed to conceal her really dangerous gift; if it had been discovered she would hardly have landed the job'. What do you think this gift was?
11   What is your assessment of Ghita's boss? (Write about 100 words in answer to this question and explain your reasons for saying what you do.)

Directed writing

1   Finish the story.
2   Ghita's headmistress complained to her boss. Decide how you think this meeting went, then write an account of the conversation they had.

Something to say

The story really begins half an hour earlier, when Nat Shelby called Lesley down from her room. When she came into the great elegant lounge, still making pin-curls and her mouth bristling with bobby pins, he put out his hand and drew her towards him.

'Les,' he said, his dark eyes watching her closely, 'your mother and I have something to tell you.' He didn't add, '– and I want you to be a strong, brave girl,' but Lesley saw those thoughts in his eyes and felt instantly alarmed.

She sat down on the brocaded arm of his chair and cuddled up to him as always. Lesley thought her father the most handsome, well-dressed and altogether marvellous man imaginable. She adored him, hung on his praise, dreaded his criticism. Not that he offered much of that. But she had always sensed in him a strangeness, something hidden and possibly dangerous – a quality of unpredictability. Deep down this feeling made her uneasy – even a little afraid of him sometimes, much as she loved him.

Across the room sat her mother. Lesley was not quite so close to her mother as to her father. Her mother knew her better than anyone in the world. They had had scenes, when her mother had crossed her, that Lesley hated to remember. It is not very pleasant, when everyone else around you thinks you are practically perfect, to have your mother know – and sometimes remind you – that you are not.

Now Miriam Shelby was smiling, but tentatively, blinking and working her bright lips nervously. This was another bad sign; she was normally so calm.

What could be wrong? Lesley tried to stiffen her inner self to receive bad news, but there wasn't much there to stiffen. In the few seconds it took her father to clear his throat and begin, Lesley's quick brain had run through several dire possibilities.

Maybe they'd decided she was too young to go to the Junior Dance with Lee? He had asked her three days ago and she had asked their permission as a matter of form.

But it was unlikely that they would change their minds on that. Though very firm in certain ways, they seldom refused her anything.

Another, more sinister possibility was that they'd somehow found out about Sonia's pot-smoking and were going to forbid Lesley to go around with her any more. They almost certainly would do so, if they knew – but how could they know? Sonia only ever did it with her cousin from Montreal, and had confided in a very shocked Lesley under a vow of utter secrecy.

The only other notion that occurred to her was that perhaps her parents had decided not to go skiing in the Rockies this Christmas. That would be awful, having to stay home for Christmas, especially as her family, being Jewish, didn't celebrate it. Most of the other Jewish families in the town made some concessions to the season, but Lesley's parents had always been very strict – ridiculously so, she thought. No party, unless she was prepared to call it a 'Hannuka Party', which would have made her feel too silly. No tree, of course, and the presents were only little Hannuka presents which didn't count (she chose to forget the big ones she got at the Jewish New Year). They did allow her to go to parties, as long as she promised not to sing carols or do anything obviously Christian.

Naturally as soon as she was out of their sight she did everything everybody else did; but she always felt bad about it, and resented feeling bad. But then after all that awful business about her brother, her father had started taking her skiing every Christmas holiday, to a Jewish resort, and that made it possible to face Christmas cheerfully.

But somehow none of these possibilities seemed likely. And indeed, all of them fell far short of the really shocking awfulness of the reality.

'Listen,' her father said at last, 'I want you to understand what I'm going to tell you.' Lesley felt a sudden coldness prickle the base of her spine. The last time he had used those words was three years ago when he had told her she must never mention her older brother's name in their family again. She sat up and took her cheek away from her father's hair.

'We're Jews,' he said (and this, too, was like that other time). 'And we're Canadians. It's becoming harder and harder to remember which should come first. My father knew, because he came from the Old Country.' The Old Country, Lesley knew, was the Ukraine. Daddy's name had once been Stupinsky, but he had changed it. 'And your mother's mother – she knew. If your mother and I had been the sort of parents they were to us, if we had kept the right sort of home for you, then what happened –' and here her father hesitated and seemed to speak with difficulty – 'What happened three years ago, wouldn't have happened.'

This was the nearest reference to Noah that had crossed either of her parents' lips since he left the house. It gave Lesley a jolt. Noah had been like one not only disgraced, but dead, and to hear her father mention him, however indirectly, was like hearing ghostly footsteps in the next room. Only a matter of the gravest importance and seriousness could make him speak like this. Lesley felt apprehension swelling in her throat; she could hardly breathe past it.

'But Daddy, you do keep a Jewish home for me! Mom cooks kosher* and all that, and you're forever telling me –'

'And you, my love, are forever shutting your ears. Jewishness is not a matter of what you're told. It's in your blood and bones. If we were doing our job right as Jewish parents, you'd be incapable of doing – a lot of the things we know very well you do.'

Lesley flushed. She was thinking guiltily of a bacon sandwich she'd eaten yesterday at Sonia's. It's hard, one of the hardest things in the world, to be different! And it's hard to accept second-hand rules, specially the food ones, like not eating pig-meat. Sometimes Lesley broke them out of sheer rebelliousness.

But clearly her father was leading up to something far more serious than bacon sandwiches.

'There's a lot more to our decision than just trying to keep you kosher,' he went on. 'Kosher's not the real point at all. I'd be prepared to give up kosher.' Lesley's mother gave a gasp of astonishment, and so did Lesley. It was as if her father had said he was prepared to give up being Nat Shelby. 'Keeping kosher is just a symbol, sometimes of something Jews forget to feel

– Jews like us who live in other people's countries.'

Lesley's bewilderment grew. 'Other people's countries? Isn't Canada our country?'

'No. Not deeply and truly. How could a Christian country be our country?'

'But there aren't any Jewish countries! Except –'

'Except Israel. And that's where we're going.'

Lesley simply couldn't take it in at first. It just wasn't possible. She gaped at her father, then turned to look at her mother. She was smiling gently and nodding, in a soothing, now don't get excited way, but her own eyes were wide with a sort of muffled panic. Was she afraid of what Lesley would now do or say, or was she – could she be afraid for herself?

Israel!

Suddenly Lesley's mind began to thaw out of its shock and look at this – this – could it be a *fact*? Could her father and mother, whom she'd always loved, trusted, and – within her limits – obeyed, really be planning to uproot them all from this safe, comfortable, happy life, and drag them all off to that outlandish place the papers were always full of? She knew very little about it, but enough to know quite definitely that it was about the last place on earth she wanted to live in. Her lip curled into an automatic grimace at the very idea.

'But – but – I was *born* here! It's my *home*!' she burst out. 'You can't expect me to leave – this house, this street, all my friends – Sonia – school – Lee – .' Each word took her deeper into strange, untrodden realms of despair, and she began to cry, her voice rising and rising. Her father tried to pull her down into his lap, but she tore away and ran to the window, keeping her back turned on them.

But the view outside of the garden, with its beautiful fiery maple tree, the hedge she often hid behind for fun when her father came home, the trim lawn where the couples had sat and held hands on her birthday ... not to mention the wide street beyond, down which, even as she looked, two of her friends came walking arm in arm, giggling over some secret – all these and a hundred other minute details so struck her to the heart that she felt she would fall to the floor and cling to the legs of the piano and defy them to tear her away.

Lynne Reid Banks *One More River*

* kosher: food prepared according to the rules of the Jewish religion. This includes a ban on any pork, bacon or ham.

Introductory work

Read the passage through and find the sentences that deal with each of these topics:
- a) The kind of life the Shelby family leads
- b) How Lesley gets on with her parents
- c) Things she tries to conceal from her parents
- d) How Lesley reacts to being Jewish

Questions

1 How did Lesley feel about her father?
2 How did she feel about her mother?
3 There are two signs that make Lesley fear that her father is about to give her bad news. What are they?
4 Lesley thinks of three possible pieces of bad news. Explain the three briefly in your own words.
5 Why is Lesley alarmed when her father says, 'I want you to understand what I'm going to tell you'?
6 What was Lesley's grandfather's surname and where had he come from?
7 What makes Lesley flush?
8 What does Lesley mean by 'second-hand rules'?
9 What do you think has happened to Noah, and what is your evidence for thinking so?
10 In this passage we are given a clear contrast between the attitudes of Lesley and her father about being Jewish. Explain this contrast in 60–80 of your own words.

Directed writing

1 Continue the conversation.
2 Lesley's parents must have thought and talked a lot before deciding to emigrate to Israel. Write a conversation between them in which they discuss it.

2. *Transitional units*

The boy

For my twelfth birthday my father promised me a box of paints.

If he behaves himself, my mother said.

I didn't say anything. Instead I did one of my famous big sniff-in sniffs. It was a case of urgent necessity.

Wipe your nose, my mother said. 5

I began counting the days to my birthday, and at the rate they went I didn't see how I'd reach my birthday this side of being an old man.

With a week to go I reckoned it was time to remind my father about the paints just in case he'd forgotten. But it turned out I didn't remind him because that afternoon after school I broke the window of the shed in our 10 backyard. It wasn't the first time either, though always an accident of course.

But the last time was almost too long ago to remember. That's how it seemed to me anyhow, though I did sort of somehow remember clearly enough that I'd been promised a thrashing the next time it happened. So I got quite a surprise when all my father did was to promise me a thrashing if 15 it happened again.

It had me properly worried. Things being what they were I didn't feel like reminding my father about the box of paints, but I thought if he could forget one promise he could just as easily forget another.

Anyhow years and years went by and one morning I woke up and found I 20 was twelve years old. It was all too marvellous for words. At breakfast my mother gave me six new handkerchiefs and said that no decent twelve year old boy ever went anywhere without a clean handkerchief in his pocket. And father told me he'd bring the box of paints when he came home from work that evening. 25

Well, that afternoon after school I was out in the backyard with my shanghai (catapult), and when I took a shot at a thrush that came and sat on our gooseberry bush you can guess what happened. My hand slipped of course.

Mother heard the noise and came to the kitchen door. You know what 30 your father said, she said, and went inside again.

When my father came home I was in my room lying on my bed. I heard him put his bike away in the shed and then I could hear him and mother talking in the kitchen. And then mother called out for me to come to my dinner. 35

I went, and my father was sitting in his place taking a look at the paper before he carved the meat. I sat down and we had dinner and I never said a word and father and mother never talked much either. And I could see the box of paints wrapped in brown paper lying on the top of the sewing machine. 40

When he'd finished his dinner my father took out his pipe and pointed.

Your paints are over there, he said.

First you can help me with the dishes, my mother said.

But I dropped the tea-towel when I saw my father light a candle and go out to put another piece of glass in the window.   45

I'll hold the candle father, I said. And here's the putty-knife father, I said.

I helped him a lot I can tell you. I helped him until he growled at me for helping him and told me to go and help my mother instead.

Later on that evening I painted a thrush in mid-air with a most painful look on its face and half its feathers flying. I told my father and mother it   50
was because I'd landed it with my shanghai.

Neither of them seemed to think much of my painting.

It's half an hour past your bedtime, my mother said.

I felt like telling her it was only twenty-five minutes, but I somehow thought with my father there I'd better not.   55

But it was only the next day that my father heard me answering my mother back, and oh gee if he didn't lay it on.

Frank Sargeson   *Tomorrow*

Introductory work

1 What kinds of fiction writing does this story include? (See pp 10–11.)
2 Make a list of the main events in the story. Number them and write them in the order in which they happened.
3 Find all the sentences about the boy's father. Make a list of all the facts we gain about him.
4 Look at the list you made for the last question and read the story again. Now write down what you can **deduce** about the boy's father and his attitude to his son. (See pp 30–33.)

Questions

1 Which sentence in the first ten lines tells us that the boy thinks it is a very long time to wait until his birthday?
2 'It had me properly worried.' (l. 17) Explain in your own words exactly why he was worried.
3 What impression do you get of the atmosphere in the family on the evening of the boy's birthday, and why?
4 Why did the boy stop helping with the washing-up?
5 How helpful do you think he was when he 'helped' his father? What makes you think this?
6 What is the point of the last line?
7 Study the passage carefully and then write three paragraphs about:
    a) the boy
    b) the mother
    c) the father.
   Make each paragraph between 50 and 100 words.

Directed writing

After the boy has gone to bed his parents talk about him. Write their conversation.

Dead bird

It is World War Two. Private Roth has just found an injured bird.

A Private Roth was completely absorbed in the bird. Each time it would open its tiny beak and try to bite his finger, he would feel a protective pang. Its entire body would flutter and vibrate from the effort, and yet there was hardly any pressure at all on his finger. Despite himself he would bring the bird up to his nose and sniff it, touching his lips against its soft feathers. Its eyes were so bright and alert. Roth had fallen in love with the bird immediately and all the frustrated affection he had stored for months seemed to pour out towards it. He fondled it and examined its injured wing tenderly. Without realizing it he was also enjoying the interest of the men who had crowded around him to look. For once he was the focus of attention.

He could not have picked a worse time to antagonize Croft.

B Sergeant Croft was sweating from the labour of making the stretcher alone: when he finished, all the difficulties of the patrol were nagging at him again. And deep within him his rage was alive again, flaring. Everything was wrong, and Roth played with a bird, while nearly half the platoon stood about watching.

His anger was too vivid for him to think. He strode across the hollow and stopped before the group around Roth.

'Jus' what do you men think you're doin'?' he asked in a low strained voice.

They all looked up, instantly wary. 'Nothin',' one of them muttered.

'Roth!'

'Yes, Sergeant?' His voice quavered.

'Give me that bird.'

C Without a word, Roth passed it to him, and Croft held it for a moment. He could feel the bird's heart beating like a pulse against his palm. Its tiny eyes darted about frantically, and Croft's anger worked into his fingertips. It would be the simplest thing to crush it in his hand: it was no bigger than a stone. He didn't know whether to smooth its soft feathers or smash it in his fingers.

'Can I have it back, Sergeant?' Roth pleaded.

The sound of his voice, already defeated, worked a spasm through Croft's fingers. He heard a little numbly the choked squeal of the bird, the sudden collapsing of its bones. It thrashed powerlessly against his palm, and the action aroused him to nausea and rage again. He felt himself hurling the bird away over the other side of the hollow, more than a hundred feet. Then his knees were left trembling.

D For a long instant no one said anything.

And then the reaction lashed about him. Ridges stood up in a fury, advanced towards Croft. 'What you doin'? . . . why'd you do that to the bird? What do ya mean. . . ?'

Goldstein, shocked and genuinely horrified, was gaping at him.

'How can you do such a thing? What harm was that bird doing you? Why did you do it? It's like . . . like. . . .' He searched for the most outrageous crime. 'It's like killing a baby.'

Croft, unconsciously, retreated a step or two. He was startled momentarily into passiveness by the force of their response.

Norman Mailer *The Naked and the Dead*

Introductory work

1 The text is printed in four sections, A, B, C, D. Write a sentence for each section describing what it is about.
2 List the people named and against each one write notes on anything we learn about him.
3 List any general information we learn about the men and who they are, where they are and what they are doing.

Questions

1 'Private Roth was completely absorbed in the bird.' Name two actions by him which showed this.
2 How did the other men react to this absorption?
3 Give two reasons, apart from the bird, why Croft was upset.
4 What phrase in section B gives a clue to the men's reaction to Croft? What do you understand by it?
5 In section C there is a sentence which shows that Croft's attitude to the bird was undecided. Quote it.
6 Explain briefly in your own words what Croft did to the bird.
7 What triggered his action?
8 How did Croft feel (a) after his action (b) after the men's reaction?
9 A number of clues are given in the text about:
   a) where the men are, what they are doing and what has been happening;
   b) the relationship between Croft and the others.
   Write a short paragraph (60–80 words) on each.

Directed writing

Write two short reports on this event, both written for a senior officer:
a) by Croft;
b) by one of the others.
Each report should be less than 100 words

A rat and some renovations

Almost every one in Ireland must have experienced American visitors or, as we called them, 'The Yanks'. Just before we were visited for the first time, my mother decided to have the working kitchen modernized. We lived in a terrace of dilapidated Victorian houses whose front gardens measured two feet by the breadth of the house. The scullery, separated from the kitchen by a wall, was the same size as the garden, and just as arable. When we pulled out the vegetable cupboard we found three or four potatoes which had fallen down behind and taken root. Ma said, 'God, if the Yanks had seen that'.

She engaged the workmen early so the job would be finished and the newness worn off by the time the Yanks arrived. She said she wouldn't like them to think that she got it done up just for them.

The first day the workmen arrived they demolished the wall, ripped up the floor and left the cold water tap hanging four feet above a bucket. We didn't see them again for three weeks. Grandma kept trying to make excuses for them, saying that it was very strenuous work. My mother however managed to get them back and they worked for three days, erecting a sink unit and leaving a hole for the outlet pipe. It must have been through this hole that the rat got in.

The first signs were discovered by Ma in the drawer of the new unit. She called me and said, 'What's those?' I looked and saw six hard brown ovals trundling about the drawer.

'Ratshit,' I said. Ma backed disbelievingly away, her hands over her mouth, repeating, 'It's mouse, it's mouse, it must be mouse.'

The man from next door, a Mr Frank Twoomey, who had lived most of his life in the country, was called – he said from the size of them, it could well be a horse. At this my mother took her nightdress and toothbrush and moved in with an aunt across the street, leaving the brother and myself with the problem. Armed with a hatchet and shovel we banged and rattled the cupboards, then when we felt sure it was gone we blocked the hole with hardboard and sent word to Ma to return, that all was well.

It was after two days' safety that she discovered the small brown bombs again. I met her with her nightdress under her arm, in the path. She just said, 'I found more,' and headed for her sister's.

That evening it was Grandma's suggestion that we should borrow the Grimley's cat. The brother was sent and had to pull it from beneath the side-board because it was very shy of strangers. He carried it across the road and the rat-killer was so terrified of traffic and Peter squeezing it that it peed all down his front. By this time Ma's curiosity had got the better of her and she ventured from her sister's to stand pale and nervous in our path. The brother set the cat down and turned to look for a cloth to wipe himself. The cat shot past him down the hall, past Ma who screamed. 'Jesus, the rat,' and leapt into the hedge. The cat ran until a bus stopped it with a thud. The Grimleys haven't spoken to us since.

Ma had begun to despair. 'What age do rats live to?' she asked. 'And what'll we do if it's still here when the Yanks come?' Peter said that they loved pigs in the kitchen.

The next day we bought stuff, pungent like phosphorous and spread it on cubes of bread. The idea of this stuff was to roast the rat inside when he ate it so that he would drink himself to death.

'Just like Uncle Matt,' said Peter. He tactlessly read out the instructions to Grandma who then came out in sympathy with the rat. Ma thought it may have gone outside, so to make sure we littered the yard with pieces of bread as well. In case it didn't work Ma decided to do a novena of masses so she got up the next morning and on the driveway to the chapel which runs along the back of our house she noticed six birds with their feet in the air, stone dead.

Later that day the rat was found in the same condition on the kitchen floor. It was quickly buried in the dustbin using the shovel as a hearse. The next day the workmen came, finished the job, and the Yanks arrived just as the paint was drying.

They looked strangely out of place with their brown, leathery faces, rimless glasses and hat brims flamboyantly large, as we met them at the boat.

... Too summery by half, against the dripping eaves of the sheds at the dockyard. At home by a roaring fire on a July day, after having laughed a little at the quaintness of the taxi, they exchanged greetings, talked about family likenesses, jobs, and then dried up. For the next half hour the conversation had to be manufactured, except for a comparison of education systems which was confusing and therefore lasted longer. Then everything stopped.

The brother said, 'I wouldn't call this an embarrassing silence'.

They all laughed, nervously dispelling the silence but not the embarrassment.

Ma tried to cover up. 'Would yous like another cup of cawfee?' Already she had begun to pick up the accent. They agreed and the oldish one with the blue hair followed her out to the kitchen.

'Gee, isn't this modern,' he said.

Ma, untacking her hand from the paint on the drawer, said, 'Yeah, we done it up last year.'

Bernard MacLaverty *Secrets*

Introductory work

1 Divide the story into five or six stages and give each one a title.
2 Make a list of all the people in the story and list any facts we learn about each one.
3 Make a list of information given in the story about (a) the house (b) the street.

Questions

1 Explain in your own words the meaning of the sentence that begins, 'The scullery, separated...'' (l. 5)
2 Why did Ma want to have the work on the kitchen finished some time before their American visitors arrived?
3 What excuse did Grandma make to explain why the workmen had not returned?
4 Why did they think that Mr Frank Twoomey would be able to help them?
5 What did the narrator and his brother try first to get rid of the rat?
6 How did the narrator know that they had not succeeded?
7 What was their next 'solution'?
8 Why was that unsuccessful?
9 What was the first sign they had that the poison they put down was effective?
10 What is the meaning of the words 'For the next half hour the conversation had to be manufactured'? (l. 66)
11 Explain in your own words the meaning of the sentence, 'They all laughed, nervously dispelling the silence but not the embarrassment.' (l. 71)
12 Explain in your own words the meaning of the following words and phrases:
    dilapidated (l. 4)   pungent (l. 47)
    tactlessly (l. 50)   flamboyantly large (l. 62)
12 What impression do you get from this story of the character of Ma, and why?

Directed writing

Write a version of this story seen through the eyes of the aunt across the street.

The box of fish

They had had a good catch of haddocks in the afternoon.

Now it was evening. In the tarred shed above the shore the four fishermen were sitting round the cold bogey stove. The oldest one kneaded the blue back of his hand with urgent knuckles.

They had not gone home after mooring the *Sea Quest* and landing the boxes of fish. Instead they had sent the boy up to the hotel for a bottle of rum on tick. 5

They could see the whirls of snow through the window of the shed.

'We just got in in time,' said Alex. He dropped a lighted match upon the driftwood and coal and paraffin in the bogey. It roared into flame at once. 10

'We'll just have one dram,' said The Partan. 'Then home for tea. The wife'll be wondering.'

The boy came in out of the darkness, empty-handed.

'Mr Blanding said, "No cash, no rum",' said the boy. '"Tell them that," said Mr Blanding. "There's more than ten pounds against The Partan on the 15 slate," he said.'

They spent more than five minutes discussing the hotelier's character in the blackest of terms.

'You see them boxes of fish,' said Tim Smith to the boy. 'Tell him, a box of haddocks for a half-bottle of rum.' 20

The boy took the box of fish in both hands and staggered out with it into the darkness.

A quarter of an hour later he was back with a half-bottle of rum.

'There's cups in the cupboard,' said a man with a black beard, Dave the skipper. 25

The boy brought over cups, darkly stained with ancient tea, and gave one each to the four fishermen round the bogey stove.

'What did you see in the village,' said The Partan to the boy. 'Did you see Mary-Ann looking for me?'

'No, I didn't,' said the boy.

Dave the skipper gravely dropped four musical measures of rum into the cups, one after the other. Rich Caribbean fragrances mingled with the smells of salt and tar. 30

'I saw two strangers,' said the boy. 'They were looking for a place for the night. They didn't look to me as if they could afford the hotel.'

Alex smacked his lips. 'There's worse things,' he said, 'than a drop of rum on a winter night.' 35

Tim set down his empty cup on the floor.

'Go and tell Mary-Ann,' said The Partan to the boy, 'I'll be home in ten minutes. Tell her we had a good catch.'

The boy went out into the night. It had stopped snowing. The sky had cleared. In at the open door stars throbbed cold and brilliant. 40

The boy was back in five minutes. Mary-Ann had told him to inform James (The Partan) that she didn't care when he came home, if ever. His tea was spoiled anyway. She would rather have the house to herself than have a poor thing of a drunk man snoring in the armchair beside the fire. She was in no hurry to see him. She had this Yule cake to bake. He would just be in the way. 45

The empty half-bottle lay on the floor.

The skipper laughed. 'Well,' he said, 'there's no hurry in that case. We deserve a drink. We've had a cold hard day of it.' 50

Three heads nodded about the ruddy stove.

The boy said he had glimpsed the two strangers between the store and the kirk. They still didn't seem to have found a place.

'Boy,' said the skipper. 'You see that box of fish against the wall. Take it up to the hotel. Mr Blanding will give you a half-bottle of rum for it. Hurry now.' 55

The top half of the bogey was red-hot. At the dark window snowflakes whirled and drifted, a horde of grey moths.

Alex licked the last drop of rum from his moustache.

At the end of half an hour the boy had still not returned. 60

'What can be keeping him?' said The Partan.

'Maybe Blanding wouldn't deal with him,' said Tim. 'Maybe Blanding thinks he's got enough fish for one night.'

They waited another ten minutes. Nobody spoke.

'What I'm feared of,' said Dave, 'is that he might have gone over the pier in the blizzard.' 65

They waited till the thick-falling snow had dwindled to a few gray loiterers under the star-flung sky; then they put on their bonnets and oilskins and blew out the lamp. It was all right – there were still five boxes of fish at the wall. They went, one after the other, up the stone steps to the village street. 70

At the hotel Mr Blanding said no, he hadn't seen the boy since the rum-fish transaction earlier in the evening.

The four fishermen went and stood at the edge of the pier looking down. It was ebb-tide. They saw no broken body on the stones surrounded by a silver scattering of fish. 75

They trooped to the boy's house. The mother opened the door to them. 'You don't need to worry,' she said. 'Sam's done exactly what you told him to do. Old Ezra's had his fish, and blind Annie, and that cripple boy at the end of the village. Who else? Sam's been at a dozen poor doors – the ones you told him to go to. At the end of it he had two fish left. He told me about the hippies or beatniks or whatever you call them – he's out now looking for them.'

'That's all right,' said the skipper. 'We were just wondering.'

Sam's mother invited them in for a drop of something, seeing it was Yule time. But they said they'd better be getting home. There was another blizzard building up in the north.

George Mackay Brown *Andrina and other stories*

Introductory work

1 Make brief notes on the **place** where the story is set.
2 Make brief notes on the **people** mentioned in the story.
3 Are there any words in the story that you do not understand? If so, list them and try to work out their meaning for yourself. (See pp 22–25.)

Questions

1 What do we learn from the story about the fishing trip the men have just returned from?
2 Why wouldn't the hotel let them have the rum on credit?
3 How do we know that the boxes of fish were heavy?
4 What is meant by the words '… dropped four musical measures of rum into the cups'? (l. 31)
5 Explain in your own words how Mary-Ann reacted to the Partan's message.
6 What indications are given in the middle section of the story that some time has passed since the men started drinking?
7 a) What is the meaning of the words in *italics* in this sentence:
      'They waited till the thick-falling snow had *dwindled to a few gray loiterers.*' (l.66)
   b) What phrase earlier in the story do these words recall?
8 What did the men expect to see when they looked over the pier?
9 Explain in your own words what the boy has done instead of going to the hotel.
10 Explain the meaning of the following words and phrases as they are used in the passage:
      dram (l.11)   bogey (l.27)   gravely (l.31)
      horde (l. 57)   the rum-fish transaction (l. 70–1)
11 In 100–150 words describe the atmosphere built up in the story and the way in which the writer achieves it.
12 What evidence is there that the story is set in a community in which people live and work closely together and know each other very well?

Directed writing

In a community such as the one in the story the news about the boy's actions would travel fast. Think about how people might react to the news and how the four fishermen might have felt about it. Now tell the story as it might have been told the next day by one villager to another.

3. *Test units*

The advocate

If you stop Ted in the street and ask him the way he is always eager to direct you. He helps the aged, the blind, the crippled. He will rescue children in distress separated from their mothers in a crowd. At the scene of an accident he is among the first to restore calm, to comfort people, ring for ambulances, distribute hot sweet tea. 5

He will reprimand or report to the police anyone making himself a public nuisance or breaking the law. Ted has deep respect for the law.

If you say good morning to him he returns your greeting with a cheerful smile.

That is Ted. 10

At work he is willing, eager; he goes out of his way to please, he stays behind in the evenings to give extra attention to his tasks and prepare for the following day. How courteous he is, how efficient.

In his conversation he refers to his many friends, to his popularity among them. 15

'They will do anything for me,' he says.

He tells you of the liftman at work who is always ready to take him to any floor, to give him service before all others; of the manager who calls him by his Christian name and gives him a friendly wink from time to time, there being definite understanding between them; of the Director who chats 20 intimately with him in a manner which he does not adopt with the other members of the staff; of the shy young office girls who are delighted to be taken 'under his wing'; of the Chief Security Officer who, relaxing the principle of keeping aloof from the staff, invites him to his room for coffee, talking to him as an equal. 25

He likes to make it known that he is given certain privileges: he is allowed

free time whenever he chooses; he is trusted, taken into the confidence of others, consulted on personal problems. He has so many friends. If you spend enough time with him you soon learn that he seems to have more friends than most people; you learn too of his illustrious relatives, of famous people who have spoken to him or corresponded with him, of high-ranking officials in other countries whom he has known intimately. In case you do not believe him (but who would doubt his word?) he has a supply of anecdotes, dates, Christian names. And in all his stories he features as the man with many friends, the man to whom people turn for advice and comfort.

Then why is he so alone? Why does he go to bed each night hoping for immediate sleep to ward off his loneliness? Why does he go every Sunday afternoon to the pictures and sit alone in the dark through two showings of the programme, and then return to his deserted flat and once more go to bed, trying to evade the loneliness?

He hasn't a friend in the world, and he knows it.

When his back is turned they label him bumptious, over-bearing, conceited, nosey-parker, poke-nose, opinionated, bigoted . . .

Over his dead body, before he is taken to be buried in the grave of a suicide, they praise him as helpful, kind, courteous, willing, conscientious, a noble and good man . . .

Which judgement is correct? Is there a correct one? How can one be judged truly, unless, like Ted, one hires the services of the Advocate Death?

Janet Frame   *You Are Now Entering the Human Heart*

Questions

1   What impression is given of Ted in the first two paragraphs?
2   What evidence is given that at work Ted is 'willing, eager'?
3   What does Ted say that the liftman, the manager, the Director and the Chief Security Officer have in common?
4   What privileges does Ted claim to have been given?
5   What evidence does Ted give of the many famous friends he has?
6   What does Ted do at weekends to try to avoid his loneliness?
7   Explain the meaning of these words as they are used in the story:
        bumptious (l. 42)   over-bearing (l. 42)
        poke-nose (l. 43)   opinionated (l. 43)
        bigoted (l. 43)
8   How did Ted die?
9   Why did people speak differently of him then?
10 When we know (a) that Ted was lonely (b) that he was disliked and (c) how he died, we may read the first part of the story differently. Find three examples of behaviour by Ted that may have been resented by others: describe them and explain why they might make him more unpopular.

Directed writing

1   Write a short conversation between two people who work with Ted in which they describe and comment on his behaviour.
2   Write two accounts of Ted by the same person: one before he died and one on the day of his funeral.

The raffle

They don't pay primary schoolteachers a lot in Trinidad, but they allow them to beat their pupils as much as they want.

Mr Hinds, my teacher, was a big beater. On the shelf below *The Last of England* he kept four or five tamarind rods. They are good for beating. They are limber, they sting and they last. There was a tamarind tree in the schoolyard. In his locker Mr Hinds also kept a leather strap soaking in the bucket of water every class had in case of fire.

It wouldn't have been so bad if Mr Hinds hadn't been so young and athletic. At the one school sports I went to, I saw him slip off his shining shoes, roll up his trousers neatly to mid-shin and win the Teachers' Hundred Yards, a cigarette between his lips, his tie flapping smartly over his shoulder. It was a wine-coloured tie: Mr Hinds was careful about his dress. That was something else that somehow added to the terror. He wore a brown suit, a cream shirt and the wine-coloured tie.

It was also rumoured that he drank heavily at weekends.

But Mr Hinds had a weak spot. He was poor. We knew he gave those 'private lessons' because he needed the extra money. He gave us private lessons in the ten-minute morning recess. Every boy paid fifty cents for that. If a boy didn't pay, he was kept in all the same and flogged until he paid.

We also knew that Mr Hinds had an allotment in Morvant where he kept some poultry and a few animals.

The other boys sympathized with us – needlessly. Mr Hinds beat us, but I believe we were all a little proud of him.

I say he beat us, but I don't really mean that. For some reason which I could never understand then and can't now, Mr Hinds never beat me. He never made me clean the blackboard. He never made me shine his shoes with the duster. He even called me by my first name, Vidiadhar.

This didn't do me any good with the other boys. At cricket I wasn't allowed to bowl or keep wicket and I always went in at number eleven. My consolation was that I was spending only two terms at the school before going on to Queen's Royal College. I didn't want to go to QRC so much as I wanted to get away from Endeavour (that was the name of the school). Mr Hinds' favour made me feel insecure.

At private lessons one morning Mr Hinds announced that he was going to raffle a goat – a shilling a chance.

He spoke with a straight face and nobody laughed. He made me write out the names of all the boys in the class on two foolscap sheets. Boys who wanted to risk a shilling had to put a tick after their names. Before private lessons ended there was a tick after every name.

I became very unpopular. Some boys didn't believe there was a goat. They all said that if there was a goat, they knew who was going to get it. I hoped they were right. I had long wanted an animal of my own, and the idea of a goat attracted me. I had heard that Mannie Ramjohn, Trinidad's champion miler, trained on goat's milk and nuts.

Next morning I wrote out the names of the boys on slips of paper. Mr Hinds borrowed my cap, put the slips in, took one out, said, 'Vidiadhar, is your goat,' and immediately threw all the slips into the wastepaper basket.

At lunch I told my mother, 'I win a goat today.'

'What sort of goat?'

'I don't know. I ain't see it.'

She laughed. She didn't believe in the goat either. But when she finished laughing she said: 'It would be nice, though.'

I was getting not to believe in the goat, too. I was afraid to ask Mr Hinds, but a day or two later he said, 'Vidiadhar, you coming, or ain't you coming to get your goat?'

He lived in a tumbledown wooden house in Woodbrook and when I got there I saw him in khaki shorts, vest and blue canvas shoes. He was cleaning his bicycle with a yellow flannel. I was overwhelmed. I had never associated him with such dress and such a menial labour. But his manner was more ironic and dismissing than in the classroom.

He led me to the back of the yard. There was a goat. A white one with big horns, tied to a plum tree. The ground around the tree was filthy. The goat looked sullen and sleepy-eyed, as if a little stunned by the smell it had made. Mr Hinds invited me to stroke the goat. I stroked it. He closed his eyes and went on chewing. When I stopped stroking him, he opened his eyes.

Every afternoon at about five an old man drove a donkey-cart through Miguel Street where we lived. The cart was piled with fresh grass tied into neat little bundles, so neat you felt grass wasn't a thing that grew but was made in a factory somewhere. That donkey-cart became important to my mother and me. We were buying five, sometimes six bundles a day, and every bundle cost six cents. The goat didn't change. He still looked sullen and bored. From time to time Mr Hinds asked me with a smile how the goat was getting on, and I said it was getting on fine. But when I asked my mother when we were going to get milk she told me to stop aggravating her. Then one day she put up a sign: 75

RAM FOR SERVICE
Apply Within For Terms

and got very angry when I asked her to explain it.

The sign made no difference. We bought the neat bundles of grass, the goat ate, and I saw no milk. 80

And when I got home one lunch-time I saw no goat.

'Somebody borrow it,' my mother said. She looked happy.

'When it coming back?'

She shrugged her shoulders.

It came back late that afternoon. When I turned the corner into Miguel 85 Street I saw it on the pavement outside our house. A man I didn't know was holding it by a rope and making a big row, gesticulating like anything with his free hand. I knew that sort of man. He wasn't going to let hold of the rope until he had said his piece. A lot of people were looking on through curtains. 90

'But why all-you want to rob poor people so?' he said, shouting. He turned to his audience behind the curtains. 'Look, all-you, just look at this goat!'

The goat, limitlessly impassive, chewed slowly, its eyes half-closed.

'But how all you people so advantageous? My brother stupid and he ain't 95 know this goat but I know this goat. Everybody in Trinidad who know about goat know this goat, from Icacos to Mayaro to Toco to Chaguaramas,' he said, naming the four corners of Trinidad. 'Is the most uselessest goat in the world. And you charge my brother for this goat? Look, you better give me back my brother money, you hear.' 100

My mother looked hurt and upset. She went inside and came out with some dollar notes. The man took them and handed over the goat.

That evening my mother said, 'Go and tell your Mr Hinds that I don't want this goat here.'

Mr Hinds didn't look surprised. 'Don't want it, eh?' He thought, and 105 passed a well-trimmed thumb-nail over his moustache. 'Look, tell you. Going to buy him back. Five dollars.'

I said, 'He eat more than that in grass alone.'

That didn't surprise him either. 'Say six, then.'

I sold. That, I thought, was the end of that. 110

One Monday afternoon about a month before the end of my last term I announced to my mother, 'That goat raffling again.'

She became alarmed.

At tea on Friday I said casually, 'I win the goat.'

She was expecting it. Before the sun set a man had brought the goat away 115 from Mr Hinds, given my mother some money and taken the goat away.

I hoped Mr Hinds would never ask about the goat. He did, though. Not the next week, but the week after that, just before school broke up.

I didn't know what to say.

But a boy called Knolly, a fast bowler and a favourite victim of Mr Hinds, 120
answered for me. 'What goat?' he whispered loudly. 'That goat kill and eat
long time.'

Mr Hinds was suddenly furious. 'Is true, Vidiadhar?'

I didn't nod or say anything. The bell rang and saved me.

At lunch I told my mother, 'I don't want to go back to that school.' 125

She said, 'You must be brave.'

I didn't like the argument, but went.

We had Geography the first period.

'Naipaul,' Mr Hinds said right away, forgetting my first name, 'define a
peninsula.' 130

'Peninsula,' I said, 'a piece of land entirely surrounded by water.'

'Good. Come up here.' He went to the locker and took out the soaked
leather strap. Then he fell on me. 'You sell my goat?' Cut. 'You kill my
goat?' Cut. 'How you so damn ungrateful?' Cut, cut, cut. 'Is the last time you
win anything I raffle.' 135

It was the last day I went to that school.

V. S. Naipaul   *The Raffle*

Questions

1   Why did Mr Hinds give private lessons and how did he force the boys to attend?
2   How did Mr Hinds show that he favoured the narrator?
3   How did the other boys react to this?
4   Why did the narrator want to win the goat?
5   Is there anything to suggest that Mr Hinds cheated over the raffle?
6   In what ways was the narrator surprised when he saw Mr Hinds at home?
7   In your own words describe the goat's appearance and behaviour.
8   Why did the narrator's mother get angry when he asked her about the milk?
9   Explain the meaning of the sign she put up.
10 Why did the man who brought the goat back complain about it?
11 Why did the narrator's mother become alarmed when she heard about the
    second goat raffle?
12 What happened to the goat in the end?
13 Why did Mr Hinds say, 'Good' when Naipaul answered his question wrongly?
14 Explain in your own words the meaning of the following words and phrases as
    they are used in the story:

    morning recess (l. 18)   insecure (l. 33)
    menial labour (l. 59)   limitlessly impassive (l. 94)
    a favourite victim (l. 120)

15 Write a character study of Mr Hinds. You should write 150–200 words and
    include in your writing comments on the following points:

    His appearance   How he behaved when crossed
    His normal behaviour at school   His private and home life

Directed writing

The narrator's mother has to talk to the headmaster about why her son is no longer
going to attend Endeavour School. (He is leaving some time before he is due to take
up a place at his new school, Queen's Royal College.) She explains her reasons for
keeping him away from school. Write the conversation that takes place.

Nuts and bolts

A The head's study

It is a traditional type of study in a building that was once part of a grammar school. **Nettleworth** *is seated behind his desk.* **Norma** *is sitting on the other side, very straight and correct with her handbag neatly on her knees.*

NETTLEWORTH: *(In his classroom voice)* ... when this school became comprehensive, I welcomed the change. Progressive, I thought ... a chance to move forward ... to break out of the academic rut. And I welcomed the girls into the classrooms. A breath of fresh air into a male, humdrum world. And so they have been. But they brought their problems ... their own prejudices and so on.

NORMA: *(Fidgeting)* Yes, but what I'm bothered about is Gaynor ...

NETTLEWORTH: I'm coming to that ...

NORMA: She seemed so normal, and then suddenly ...

NETTLEWORTH: Normal?

NORMA: That's right.

NETTLEWORTH: She was a very bored young lady.

NORMA: Because she hadn't enough to occupy her mind. I said that to her all along ...

NETTLEWORTH: And now she has got something to occupy her mind.

NORMA: Nuts and silly bolts!

NETTLEWORTH: Exactly. She will make a very good mechanic.

NORMA: *(Staring at him)* You mean you like what she's doing?

NETTLEWORTH: I think she's found her niche.

NORMA: But what about her future?

NETTLEWORTH: She must make her future for herself.

NORMA: *(Crossly)* With nuts and bolts, I suppose?

NETTLEWORTH: Precisely. *(Slight pause.* **Norma** *is defeated momentarily)* I am trying, in this school, to open up new horizons for the young people. You see, in spite of Women's Lib and all that, boys will be boys and –

NORMA: Girls should be girls! She hasn't a stitch of clothing to her back which isn't covered with oil ...

NETTLEWORTH: Surely that isn't ...

NORMA: I have to wash them, don't I? And I want her to look nice ...

NETTLEWORTH: Why?

(Pause)

NORMA: Every mother wants her daughter to look nice ...

NETTLEWORTH: We are living in revolutionary times, Mrs Potts, and we must try to move with them.

NORMA: I'm not interested in revolutions, Mr Nettleworth.

NETTLEWORTH: There are those of us who are aware of the limitations being thrust upon us by society ... *(He stands up and moves about the room as if lecturing)* I try to encourage the girls and boys to realize their own special potential. To get away from their textbook image. I want the boys to nurse the baby, and the girls to drive in the nails, if they fancy it. It is an uphill battle ...

NORMA: *(Cutting in, very much on her dignity. Her lips pursed)* I would like you to speak to Gaynor, Mr Nettleworth, and persuade her to see sense. That's all I came about. I don't want to be lectured. I can't see her ever realizing her potential while she's covered from head to foot in oil.

NETTLEWORTH: *(He is about to say something, but then feels it is futile. He moves to the door and opens it for* **Norma***)* Thank you for coming. *(Very politely)* I like to see parents as often as possible. Very helpful if the young people have problems.

NORMA: *(A little mollified)* Good morning.

B The Pottses' living room

It is evening. The curtains are closed. **George** *and*
Norma *sit side by side on the settee watching
television, which they do in a mesmerized fashion.*
Norma *is knitting.*

NORMA: I've told her ... it's got to stop. *(Slight
pause)* I said to her, 'Gaynor, these are my last
words on the subject. You give up this
ridiculous business of bicycles in the bedroom
or ...'

GEORGE: *(Mildly surprised)* Or?

NORMA: Well ... she'd have to go?

GEORGE: You don't mean that. How can she go?
(Slight pause) She's under age.

NORMA: Well, something must be done. I'm not
having it any more, George. I'm not as young
as I was. I can't cope with revolutions at my
age, and I don't see why I should be expected
to. She's just got to get back to normal.

C The head's study

Nettleworth *is seated behind his desk. On the
other side is* **Gaynor**.

NETTLEWORTH: I suppose you could get down to
thinking of something realistic; something
accepted more readily as a job for you ... like
librarian?

GAYNOR: Realistic, I thought you said.

NETTLEWORTH: Yes. I did.

GAYNOR: Doesn't sound realistic to me.

NETTLEWORTH: No. *(Slight pause)* How's the
bicycle building going?

GAYNOR: Progressing.

NETTLEWORTH: A good word that.

GAYNOR: Yeh?

NETTLEWORTH: One that I'm rather fond of.

GAYNOR: Mum's throwing it out.

NETTLEWORTH: The bike?

GAYNOR: Yeh. She doesn't like it in the bedroom.

NETTLEWORTH: Yes ... well I can hardly blame
her for that.

GAYNOR: It's an excuse. If the place was littered with sewing machines and that lot, she wouldn't turn a hair.

NETTLEWORTH: Why not build a sewing machine?

GAYNOR: Not realistic. You need fine tools and all that. And I don't like sewing machines; too fiddly altogether. I like my bike. I'm doing very well with it. Got lots of bits from the scrap man. And he's got an ancient one in now that I'm going to break down.

NETTLEWORTH: Sounds good.

GAYNOR: (Wistfully) I need a workshop though.

NETTLEWORTH: No shed in the backyard?

GAYNOR: No backyard. (Slight pause)

NETTLEWORTH: (Smiling) An outside lav going spare somewhere?

GAYNOR: Never thought of that.

NETTLEWORTH: Somewhere there is a place just waiting to be found. I'm sure of that. (A bell rings somewhere in the school) There we are then.

GAYNOR: (Rising. She looks depressed. She moves to the door where she hesitates with her hand on the knob. She stares down at the knob) Maybe I should be a librarian.

NETTLEWORTH: It ... would be a lot easier, of course. (Slight pause) And I should advise you to do just that. Shouldn't I?

GAYNOR: See you! (She goes out)

NETTLEWORTH: (Quietly) See you!

D Interior of a small shed

It is gloomy. The only light comes through a gap in the boarded-up window. There is a lavatory with cast iron cistern in one corner. The shed contains a well-littered workbench, some timber, old car number plates, etc., and a general clutter of tools, bits of machinery, etc. Most of this is now junk and much of it is rusty. The door creaks open about half way. More light comes in. **John** *enters.*

JOHN: Well, this is it. Pretty small.

GAYNOR: (Squeezing in after him) Not bad.

JOHN: My old man had his little workshop here. But I never used it. I need more space. He repaired bikes, of course. Lots of bikes in those days.

GAYNOR: (Moving around examining the place) Yeh.

JOHN: I moved on to cars – naturally. I like a good car.

GAYNOR: So do I.

JOHN: So this place ... I just keep a few odd tools here ... and, like, the lavatory. What do you want it for, eh? Some sort of club? (Slight pause) I can't have any carrying on, Gaynor. (Slight pause) I'd have your mum after me, it –

GAYNOR: How much do you want for the use of it?

JOHN: I've never given it any thought.

GAYNOR: Fifty pence a week?

JOHN: (A bit bemused) Well ...

GAYNOR: Go on. Say 'yes'.

JOHN: But what d'you want it for, girl?

GAYNOR: A workshop, of course.

JOHN: For you?

GAYNOR: Yeh.

JOHN: (Suspicious) To work at what? You young people get up to all sorts ... I don't know ...

GAYNOR: Come off it, Uncle John. You know me … And Mum says she'll throw me out.

JOHN: Eh? You're not going to live here?

GAYNOR: Heck, no! *(She goes very grown up)* I'm working on a small engineering project. Mum doesn't like it in the house. I mean to expand. I've a lot to learn. *(A thought strikes her)* Do you want an odd jobber in your garage?

JOHN: An odd jobber?

GAYNOR: Yeah.

JOHN: You could go on the petrol pump.

GAYNOR: No, I want to help with the cars.

JOHN: Now I know you're hare-brained …

GAYNOR: If I did some work for you, maybe you could give me some old parts you don't want; then I could break them down … learn about them. Please. I'm a good worker.

JOHN: Well, I don't …

GAYNOR: Let me come of a Saturday. I'll work for nothing. You won't regret it.

JOHN: What'll I do with a girl under my feet all day? And what about the lavatory?

GAYNOR: You've got another lav, I can move out if anyone wants to come in here. I'll take over this shed tomorrow night and start work in the garage on Saturday morning, eh? Eight-thirty, isn't it?

JOHN: No. No, you can't.

GAYNOR: Oh, come on …

JOHN: No. I can't have you messing about in my garage. Folks'll wonder what I'm up to. No, Gaynor. You can go on the pumps like the other girls.

GAYNOR: I'll go on the pumps, then. *(She moves to the door.* **John** *opens it wider for her)* For the time being.

Julia Jones   *Nuts and Bolts*

Questions

1 Explain what the school had been and what it has become.
2 What does Norma mean by 'normal' for a girl?
3 What does Nettleworth mean by 'I think she's found her niche'?
4 What does he mean when he says he wants boys and girls 'To get away from their text book image'?
5 Explain the meaning of the stage direction describing Norma as '*A little mollified*, (Scene A).
6 What weakness does George reveal in Norma's position in Scene B?
7 What do we learn in Scene C about what Gaynor is doing in her bedroom?
8 What two reasons does she give for rejecting the idea of working on sewing machines?
9 How does the writer make a link between the end of Scene C and the beginning of Scene D?
10 Who is John (Scene D)?
11 Why is he suspicious of Gaynor?
12 Why won't he let her help with the cars?
13 Describe the characters of Gaynor and Norma as presented in these scenes.
14 The scenes illustrate a number of different attitudes towards the role of women in society. Write 150–200 words outlining the main attitudes expressed.

Directed writing

Think about the attitudes expressed towards Gaynor and her ambitions by
(a) Norma (b) John. Imagine what they might say to each other when Norma finds out about the arrangement between Gaynor and John. Write the conversation they have.

Christian endeavour

I had been a religious fanatic for only a few weeks.

'What is it the night then?' asked my father. 'The bandy hope?' I caught the mockery, but he meant no harm.

'Christian Endeavour,' I said, drying my face with a towel and stretching up to peer at myself in the cracked mirror above the sink. 'Band a Hope's on Thursday.'

The two halves of my face in the mirror didn't quite match because of the crack, were slightly out of alignment. It was an old shaving-mirror of my father's with an aluminium ring, hung squint from a nail in the window-frame.

'Ah thought Christian Endeavour was last night?'

'That was just the Juniors,' I said. 'Tonight's the Real one.'

'Are ye no too young?' said my father.

'The minister says ah can come.'

'Is that because ye were top in the bible exam?'

'Top equal,' I said. 'Ah don't know if that's why. He just said ah could come.'

'Ach well,' said my father, going back behind his newspaper. 'Keeps ye aff the streets.'

'Ah'll be the youngest there,' I said, proud of myself and wanting to share it.

'Mind yer heid in the door,' he said. 'It's that big ye'll get stuck.'

I pulled on my jacket and was ready to go.

'Seen ma bible?' I asked.

'Try lookin where ye left it,' he said.

I found it on the table with another book, *The life of David Livingstone*, under the past week's heap of newspapers and comics. The book had been my prize in the bible exam.

The exam had been easy. Questions like *Who carried Christ's cross on the way to Calvary?* And from the Shorter Catechism, *Into what estate did the fall bring mankind?*

It was just a matter of remembering.

The label gummed in the book read FIRST PRIZE, with EQUAL penned in above BIBLE KNOWLEDGE, and then my name.

My father remembered reading the same book as a boy. He had been a sergeant in the Boys' Brigade, and the book had made him want to be a missionary himself.

'Great White Doctor an that,' he said. 'Off tae darkest Africa.'

But somehow he had drifted away from it all. 'Wound up in darkest Govan instead,' he said.

For the years he had been in the Boys' Brigade, he had been given a long-service badge. I still kept it in a drawer with a hoard of other badges I had gathered over the years. Most of them were cheap tin things, button badges: ABC Minors, Keep Britain Tidy. But the BB badge was special, heavier metal in the shape of an anchor. I had polished it with Brasso till it shone. There were two other treasures in the drawer: an army badge an uncle had given me, shaped like a flame, and a Rangers supporters badge, a silver shield with the lion rampant in red.

Christian Endeavour had a badge of its own. A dark blue circle with a gold rim, and CE in gold letters. The Sunday-school teachers at the Mission all wore it. I had been disappointed that there wasn't one for the Juniors. But now that I was moving up, I would be entitled to wear the badge. CE. In Gold.

'Is ther gonnae be any other youngsters there the night?' asked my father.

'Jist Norman,' I said. Norman was the minister's son. He was twelve, a year older than me.

'Ye don't like him, do ye?'

'He's a big snotter,' I said. 'Thinks e's great.'

'Wis he top in the bible exam as well?'

'Top equal,' I said. My father laughed.

'That minister's quite a nice wee fella,' he said. 'That time he came up here, after yer mother died, we had quite a wee chat.'

'Aye, ye told me,' I said.

'Ah think he got a surprise. Wi me no goin tae church an that, he must thought ah was a bitty a heathen. Expected tae find me aw bitter, crackin up y'know.'

'Aye, ah know.'

'But ah wisnae. Ah showed um ma long-service badge fae the BB. Even quoted scripture at him!'

'Aye.'

'"In my father's house there are many mansions" ah said. That's the text they read at the funeral.'

'Time ah was goin.' I said.

'He wanted me tae come tae church,' said my father. 'But ah cannae be bothered wi aw that. Anywey, you're goin enough for the two ae us these days, eh?'

'Aye. Cheerio, da.'

'See ye after, son.'

I took a last look at my reflection in the squinty mirror.

'Right,' I said.

I took the shortcut to the Mission, across the back courts. It was already dark, and in the light from the windows I could make out five or six boys in the distance. From their noise I could recognize them as my friends, and I hurried on, not really wanting them to see me. If they asked where I was going, they would only mock.

I hadn't been out with them this week, except for playing football after school. They thought I was soft in the head for going so much to the Mission. They couldn't understand. I felt a glow. It was good to feel good. It had come on stronger since my mother had died. The Mission was a refuge from the empty feeling of lack.

But part of me was always drawn back to my friends, to their rampaging and their madness.

I heard a midden-bin being overturned, a bottle being smashed, and the gang of boys scattered laughing through the backs as somebody shouted after them from a third-storey window. Head down, I hurried through a close and out into the street.

Now that I was almost at the Mission, I felt nervous and a little afraid. I had never been to an adult meeting before. I thought of the lapel-badge with the gold letters. CE. Perhaps I would even be given one tonight. Initiated. There was another badge I had seen the teachers wearing. It was green with a gold lamp, an oil lamp like Aladdin's. But maybe that was only for ministers and teachers.

Give me oil in my lamp. Keep me burning.
Give me oil in my lamp I pray.
Halleluja!

The Mission hall was an old converted shop, the windows covered over with corrugated iron. A handwritten sign on the door read CHRISTIAN ENDEAVOUR. Tonight. 7.30. I stood for a moment, hesitating, outside. Then I pushed open the door and went in to the brightness and warmth.

I was early, and only a handful of people had arrived. They sat, talking, in a group near the front of the hall, and nobody seemed to have noticed me come in.

Norman was busy stacking hymn-books. Looking up, he saw me and nodded, then went out into the back room.

The minister saw me and waved me over. There were two or three earnest conversations going on. The minister introduced me to a middle-aged African couple.

'These are our very special guests,' he said. 'Mr and Mrs Lutula.'

'How do you do,' we all said, and very formally shook hands. There was a momentary lull then the conversations picked up again. But I could feel the big black woman looking at me.

'And tell me,' she said, her voice deep like a man's, 'when did the Lord Jesus come into your heart?'

'Pardon?' I said, terrified.

'Ah said, when did the Lord Jesus come into your heart, child?'

That was what I thought she had said. And she wanted an answer. From me. I looked up at the broad face smiling at me, the dark eyes shining. I looked down at the floor. I could feel myself blush. What kind of question was that to ask? How was I supposed to answer it?

Why didn't she ask me something straightforward?

Who carried Christ's cross on the way to Calvary?
Joseph of Aramathea.
Into what estate did the fall bring mankind?
The fall brought mankind into an estate of sin and misery.

I sat, tense and rigid, on the hard wooden seat. Now my face was really hot and flushed. I cleared my throat. In a squeak of a voice I said, 'I don't know if . . .'

I look at the floor.

She leaned over and patted my arm. 'Bless you, child,' she said, smiling, and turned to talk to her husband.

I stood up, still looking at the floor. I made my way, conscious of every step, clumsy and awkward, to the back of the hall and out into the street. I walked faster; I began to run, away from the Mission, along the street, through the close into the back court.

The night air cooled me. I stopped and leaned against a midden wall. I was in absolute misery, tortured by my own sense of foolishness. It wasn't just the question, it was what it had opened up; a realm where I knew nothing, could say nothing.

When did the Lord Jesus come into my heart? I could have said it was when my mother died. That would have sounded pious. But I didn't think it was true. I didn't know. That was it; I didn't know. If the Lord Jesus had come into my heart, I should know.

And how could I go back in now? It was all too much for me. I would tell the minister on Sunday I had felt hot and flushed, had gone outside for some air. That much was true. I would say I had felt sick and gone home.

The back court was quiet. There was no sound, except for the TV from this house or that. Bright lit windows in the dark tenement blocks. I walked on, slow, across the back, and as I passed another midden, I kicked over a bin and ran.

Nearer home I slowed down again.

My father would ask why I was back so early.

Alan Spence

Questions

1 What do you suppose 'The bandy hope' is?
2 What meeting is the narrator attending that night?
3 Why does his father criticize him for being big-headed?
4 Where do they live?
5 What is the importance of the Christian Endeavour badge to the boy?
6 In what two ways did the father surprise the minister?
7 Why did the boy not want his friends to see him on his way to the Mission?
8 How had his feeling about the Mission changed since his mother died?
9 How did Mrs Lutula's question affect the narrator?
10 What excuse did he plan for leaving the hall?
11 Why did he want to delay meeting his father again?
12 Write about 75–100 words describing and commenting on the boy's relationship with his father.
13 What would you say were the boy's real motives for his regular attendance at the meetings of Christian Endeavour?
14 Why was he unable to answer Mrs Lutula's question and why did it make him feel so bad?

Directed writing

Write an account of the conversation that takes place when he gets home.

The village that lost its children

Few people had ever heard of Aberfan until disaster struck it. It was just another of the small mining ghettoes lying tucked away in the sump of the South Wales valleys – a huddle of anonymous terraced houses of uniform ugliness unrelieved except for chapel and pub.

Its heart was the coal-pit, and its environment like the others – the debris of a slowly exhausting industry: a disused canal, some decaying rail-tracks, a river black as the Styx, a general coating of grime over roofs and gardens, and the hills above blistered with a century of slag-heaps.

Such villages learned to accept a twilight world where most of the menfolk worked down the pits. Many died early, with their lungs full of coal-dust, and the life was traditionally grim and perilous. Disaster, in fact, was about the only news that ever came out of the valleys – the sudden explosion underground, miners entombed alive, or the silent death in the dark from gas. Wales and the world were long hardened to such news. But not to what happened in Aberfan...

A colliery sends to the surface more waste than coal, and a mining village has to learn to live with it. It must be put somewhere or the mine would close, and it's too expensive to carry it far. So the tips grow everywhere, straddling the hillsides, nudging the houses like black-furred beasts. Almost everyone, from time to time, has seen danger in them, but mostly they are endured as a fact of life.

On the mountain above Aberfan there were seven such tips. The evening sun sank early behind them. To some of the younger generation they had always been there, as though dumped by the hand of God. They could be seen from the school windows, immediately below them, rising like black pyramids in the western sky. But they were not as solid as they looked; it was known that several had moved in the past, inching ominously down the mountain.

What was not known however was that the newest tip, number 7, was a killer with a rotten heart. It had been begun in Easter 1958, and was built on a mountain spring, most treacherous of all foundations. Gradually, over the years, the fatal seeping of water was turning Tip 7 into a mountain of moving muck.

Then one morning, out of the mist, the unthinkable happened, and the tip came down on the village. The children of Pantglas Junior School had just arrived in their classroom and were right in the path of it. They were the first to be hit by the wave of stupefying filth which instantly smothered more than a hundred of them.

The catastrophe was not only the worst in Wales but an event of such wanton and indifferent cruelty it seemed to put to shame both man and God...

The tragedy of Aberfan was one of inertia – of a danger which grew slowly for all to see, but which almost no one took steps to prevent. Now that the worst has happened, the process of healing also seems infected by the inertia of public authority and private grief – a dullness of shock and apathy which freezes the power of action.

Even today, a year later, the visitor needn't search hard for reminders; the

stain of what happened is still nakedly visible. One sees the ineffectual little
bulldozers, high on the mountain, patting and smoothing the remains of the
tip. The black trail down the hillside left behind by the avalanche – a series   50
of gigantic descending waves – is now covered by the fresh false innocence of
grass which doesn't conceal its revolting power.

Where the waves broke on the village remains a terrible void, and little has
been done to soften its horror. Sheered-off houses, broken walls and polluted
back-gardens, a heap of smashed and rusty cars; these form a rim of
wreckage around a central wilderness – the site where the school once stood.

Immediately after the disaster, in a kind of frenzy of outrage, all that was
left of the school buildings was savagely bulldozed. It seems to have been the
last attempt to obliterate the pain. The scene of the tragedy today, where a
hundred and sixteen children died, is just a sloping area of squalid rubbish, a   60
trodden waste – lying derelict in the rain.

Someone, over the months, has aimlessly tried to enclose it with a few old
railings and bits of broken wire. The barrier is ineffective and almost obscene
and only stresses the desolation. Walk across the site and the ground itself
seems stifled, choked and littered with trash – old shoes, stockings, lengths of
iron piping, lemonade cartons, rags. Fragments of the school itself still lie
embedded in the rubbish – chunks of green-painted classroom wall – all

gummed together by the congealed slime of the tip and reeking sourly of
sulphurous ash.

Even more poignant relics lie in a corner of the buried playground, piled   70
haphazardly against a wall – some miniature desks and chairs, evocative as a
dead child's clothes, infant-sized, still showing the shape of their bodies.
Among the rubble there also lie crumpled little song-books, sodden and
smeared with slime, the words of some bed-time song still visible on the
pages surrounded by drawings of sleeping elves.

Across the road from the school, and facing up the mountain, stands a
row of abandoned houses. This must once have been a trim little working-
class terrace, staidly Victorian but specially Welsh, with lace-curtained
windows, potted plants in the hall, and a piano in every parlour – until the
wave of slag broke against it, smashed in the doors and windows, and   80
squeezed through the rooms like toothpaste.

Something has been done to clear them, but not very much. They stand
like broken and blackened teeth. Doors sag, windows gape, revealing the
devastation within – a crushed piano, some half-smothered furniture. You
can step in from the street and walk round the forsaken rooms which still
emit an aura of suffocation and panic – floors scattered with letters, coat-
hangers on the stairs, a jar of pickles on the kitchen table. The sense of
catastrophe and desertion, resembling the choked ruins of Pompeii, hangs in
the air like volcanic dust.

But the raw, naked, inexplicable scar on the village remains the site of the   90
school itself – that festering waste of sombre silence from which no one can
take their eyes. Why, one wonders, after all this time, has it not been cleared
or decently covered? It seems that the people of Aberfan are made powerless
by it, spellbound, unable to move. The ground is so seared with memory it
has become a kind of no-man's-land, a negative limbo paralysing the will,
something poisoned, sterile and permanently damned, on which nothing can
be planted, nothing built.

The aftertaste of the macabre which still affects the village is strengthened
further by its attraction for sightseers. The streets of Aberfan are narrow,
and not built for traffic, so the bulldozed site of the Junior School itself has   100
become the most convenient carpark for tourists. Almost any fine afternoon
you will see them arrive, parents and children with cameras and balloons,
clambering over the ruins and up and down the railway embankment eating
ice-creams and photographing each other.

I remember young lovers arm-in-arm wandering around the devastated
waste; a green-suited blonde posing against a slag-heap; another in shorts
hitching a ride on a bulldozer; an elegant old lady poking at pieces of rubble.

They had come, they had seen it – the shock of Aberfan for an outing, to
take home with their snaps and seaweed. Visitors from America, Canada and
Australia, too, tip-toeing carefully with large round eyes. With a certain   110
eagerness also exclaiming, 'My, wasn't it just terrible?' Approaching a miner
with a hushed enquiry. 'Excuse me, please,' – pointing down – 'but are they
still under there? . . .' 'What was it like – were you here that day?'

Most of the villagers seem in no way distressed by this, visitors are a
comfort rather than an intrusion. The stories begin again for each newcomer,
recited in a kind of dream.

... Yet the trippers, scrambling over the slag in their bright holiday clothes, are on the whole not a lovely sight. As one old miner exclaimed, 'Why don't they bring their buckets and spades? There's plenty of dirt for them to dig.'

120

But some of the Welsh visitors, one notices – those from the neighbouring coal-valleys – are subtly different from any of the others.

They come in silent families, without questions or cameras, but bring their children too – walking them quickly over the ruins and hold on to their arms, feeling their living flesh ...

Laurie Lee   *I Can't Stay Long*

Questions

1   What does the writer say are the typical features of a South Wales mining village?
2   What evidence does the third paragraph give that mining is dangerous?
3   Why are there always tips round coal mines?
4   What caused tip number 7 at Aberfan to be unstable?
5   What does the writer mean by the words 'The tragedy of Aberfan was one of inertia ...?' (l. 42)
6   In what ways, according to the writer is inertia still affecting Aberfan?
7   Why does the writer think that the remains of the school buildings were demolished after the disaster?
8   To what does he compare the school desks, and why?
9   Why does he compare the deserted houses to the ruins of Pompeii?
10   He describes two types of visitor to the village. What are they?
11   Describe briefly in 50–80 of your own words what happened at Aberfan and why?
12   The writer describes and comments on the village's own reaction to the disaster. Summarize what he says in about 100 words.
13   What are the writer's own reactions to his visit to Aberfan? Describe it in your own words.

Directed writing

The writer notes that the visitors are eager to ask questions about the tragedy and the villagers are willing to talk about it. Using the information in the text and your own imagination, reconstruct in your own mind what the disaster must have been like. Now write a conversation between a visitor and a villager about the event.

Unreliable memoirs

School, passable for the first year, became unbearable in the second, when
kind Miss Dear was supplanted by a hard case called Miss Turnbull. Dark,
cold and impatient, Miss Turnbull might have been the firm hand I needed,
but already I was unable to cope with authority. I still can't today, tending
to oscillate between nervous flippancy and overly solicitous respect. In those   5
days, when I was about a third of my present height and a quarter of the
weight, there was nothing to do except duck. I did everything to get out of
facing up to Miss Turnbull. I had Mondayitis every day of the week. As
my mother dragged me down the front path, I would clutch my stomach,
cross my eyes, stick out my tongue, cough, choke, scream and vomit   10
simultaneously.

But there were some occasions when I ended up at school no matter what
I did. It was then revealed that I had Dropped Behind the Class. Words I
could not recognize would come up on the spelling wheel. The spelling wheel

was a thick card with a window in it and a cardboard disc behind. As you   15
turned the disc, words appeared one at a time in the window. I remember not
being able to pronounce the word 'the'. I pronounced it 'ter-her'. The class
had collective hysterics. They were rolling around on the floor with their
knees up. I suppose one of the reasons why I grew up feeling the need to
cause laughter was perpetual fear of being its unwitting object.   20

From the start of Miss Turnbull's reign until the day we left Jannali, every
morning I would shout the house down. For my mother, the path leading
from the front porch to the front gate became a Via Dolorosa*. My act
reached ever new heights of extravagance. Either it worked or it didn't. If
it didn't I would sit in school praying for the bushfires to come early and   25
incinerate the place. If it did I would either hang around the house or go and
play with Ron, a truant of my own age who lived next to Hally the butcher
down near the station. Ron was a grub. I was always being warned off him
because he was so filthy.

Ron's wreck of a mother used to give us buttered bread with hundreds and   30
thousands on it. It was like being handed a slice of powdered rainbow. They
must have been a poor family but I remember my visits to them as luxuries.
As well as the Technicolor bread and butter, there were vivid, viscid green
drinks made from some kind of cordial. Ron's place would have been Beulah
Land* except for one drawback. They had a cattle dog called Bluey. A   35
known psychopath, Bluey would attack himself if nothing else was available.
To avert instant death, I was supposed to call out from the front gate when I
arrived and not open it until I was told that Bluey had been chained up. One
day I opened it too early and Bluey met me on the front path. I don't know
where he had come from – probably around the side of the house – but it   40
was as if he had come up out of the ground on a lift. He was nasty enough
when chained up but on the loose he was a bad dream. Barking from the
stomach, he opened a mouth like a great, wet tropical flower. When he
snapped it shut, my right foot was inside it.

If Bluey hadn't been as old as the hills, my foot would have come right off.   45
Luckily his teeth were in ruins, but even so I was only a few tendons short of
becoming an amputee. Since Bluey's spittle obviously contained every
bacterium known to science, my frantic mother concluded that the local
doctor would not be enough. I think I went to some kind of hospital in
Sutherland. Needles were stuck into me while she had yet another case of   50
heart failure. Bluey was taken away to be destroyed. Looking back on it, I
can see that this was tough on Bluey, who had grown old in the belief that
biting ankles was the thing to do. At the time I was traumatized. I loathed
dogs from that day forward. They could sense my terror from miles away.
Any dog could back me against a wall for hours. Eventually I learned not to   55
show fear. The breakthrough came when I managed to walk away from a
dog who had me bailed up against the door of a garage. Admittedly he was
only a Pekinese about eight inches long, but it was still a triumph. That was
more than a year ago.

Such incidents must have been hell on my mother's nerves. I would have   60
been enough of a handful even in normal circumstances but the sweat of
looking after me was made worse by her uncertainty about what was
happening to my father. She got some news of him when he was in Changi*

but after he was moved to Japan there was not much to go on. The mail from Kobe, when there was any, was so censored it looked like shredded lettuce. During the last part of the war she wasn't even certain that he was alive. In those circumstances it couldn't have been much help to her, having the kind of son who goes off and gets half-eaten by a dog.

Clive James   *Unreliable Memoirs*

* Via Dolorosa: the route followed by Christ on his way to being crucified, and hence any grievous or distressing experience.
* Beulah Land: the land of Israel in the Old Testament.
*Changi: Japanese prisoner-of-war camp in Malaya, where many Australian and British soldiers were held.

Questions

1   How and why did school change for the author in the second year?
2   Explain what is meant by the words, 'tending to oscillate between nervous flippancy and overly solicitous respect'. (l. 5)
3   What does he mean by 'Mondayitis'? (l. 8)
4   Explain in your own words why he now likes to make people laugh.
5   Describe what the author used to do to avoid going to school.
6   What was he supposed to do when visiting Ron's house?
7   What effects did being bitten by Bluey have on his attitude to dogs?
8   Where was the author's father during all this time, and why?
9   Explain in your own words the meanings of the words and phrases:
       collective hysterics (l. 18)   a grub (l. 28)   viscid (l. 33)
       a known psychopath (l. 36)   amputee (l. 47)
10   What impression do you get of each of the following characters:
       Miss Turnbull
       Ron's mother
       The author's mother
11   This story is entertaining because Clive James remembers particular incidents with vivid clarity. Choose two details that illustrate this and explain why you have chosen them.

Directed writing

1   Write Miss Turnbull's final school report on Clive James.
2   Presumably the author's mother used to write to her husband giving him the news of what was happening at home. How much of what was really going on would she have told him? Write the letter that she might have written shortly after the incident with Bluey.

The golden kite, the silver wind

'In the shape of a *pig?*' cried the Mandarin.

'In the shape of a pig,' said the messenger, and departed.

'Oh, what an evil day in an evil year,' cried the Mandarin. 'The town of Kwan-Si, beyond the hill, was very small in my childhood. Now it has grown so large that at last they are building a wall.'

'But why should a wall two miles away make my good father sad and angry all within the hour?' asked his daughter quietly.

'They build their wall,' said the Mandarin, 'in the shape of a pig! Do you see? Our own city wall is built in the shape of an orange. That pig will devour us, greedily!'   10

'Ah.'

They both sat thinking.

Life was full of symbols and omens. Demons lurked everywhere. Death swam in the wetness of an eye, the turn of a gull's wing meant rain. A fan held so, the tilt of a roof, and, yes, even a city wall was of immense importance. Travellers and tourists, caravans, musicians, artists, coming upon these two towns, equally judging the portents, would say, 'The city shaped like an orange? No! I will enter the city shaped like a pig and prosper, eating all, growing fat with good luck and prosperity!'

The Mandarin wept. 'All is lost! These symbols and signs terrify. Our city   20
will come on evil days.'

'Then,' said the daughter, 'call in your stonemasons and temple builders. I will whisper from behind the silken screen and you will know the words.'

The old man clapped his hands despairingly. 'Ho, stonemasons! Ho, builders of towns and palaces!'

The men who knew marble and granite and onyx and quartz came quickly. The Mandarin faced them most uneasily, himself waiting for a whisper from the silken screen behind his throne. At last the whisper came.

'I have called you here,' said the whisper.

'I have called you here,' said the Mandarin aloud, 'because our city is   30
shaped like an orange, and the vile city of Kwan-Si has this day shaped theirs like a ravenous pig –'

Here the stonemasons groaned and wept. Death rattled his cane in the outer courtyard. Poverty made a sound like a wet cough in the shadows of the room.

'And so,' said the whisper, like the Mandarin, 'you raisers of walls must go bearing trowels and rocks and change the shape of our city!'

The architects and masons gasped. The Mandarin himself gasped at what he had said. The whisper whispered. The Mandarin went on: 'And you will change our walls into a club which may beat the pig and drive if off!'   40

The stonemasons rose up, shouting. Even the Mandarin, delighted at the words from his mouth, applauded, stood down from his throne. 'Quick!' he cried. 'To work!'

When his men had gone, smiling and bustling, the Mandarin turned with great love to the silken screen. 'Daughter,' he whispered, 'I will embrace you.' There was no reply. He stepped around the screen, and she was gone.

Such modesty, he thought. She has slipped away and left me with a
triumph, as if it were mine.

The news spread through the city; the Mandarin was acclaimed. Everyone
carried stone to the walls. Fireworks were set off and the demons of death   50
and poverty did not linger, as all worked together. At the end of the month
the wall had been changed. It was now a mighty bludgeon with which to
drive pigs, boars, even lions, far away. The Mandarin slept like a happy fox
every night.

'I would like to see the Mandarin of Kwan-Si when the news is learned.
Such pandemonium and hysteria; he will likely throw himself from a
mountain! A little more of that wine, oh Daughter-who-thinks-like-a-son.'

But the pleasure was like a winter flower; it died swiftly. That very
afternoon, the messsenger rushed into the courtroom. 'Oh Mandarin,   60
disease, early sorrow, avalanches, grasshopper plagues, and poisoned well
water!'

The Mandarin trembled.

'The town of Kwan-Si,' said the messenger, 'which was built like a pig and
which animal we drove away by changing our wall to a mighty stick, has
now turned triumph to winter ashes. They have built their city's walls like a
great bonfire to burn our stick!'

The Mandarin's heart sickened within him, like an autumn fruit upon the
ancient tree. 'Oh, gods! Travellers will spurn us. Tradesmen, reading the
symbols, will turn from the stick, so easily destroyed, to the fire, which   70
conquers all!'

'No,' said a whisper like a snowflake from behind the silken screen.

'No,' said the startled Mandarin.

'Tell my stonemasons,' said the whisper that was a falling drop of rain, 'to

build our walls in the shape of a shining lake.'

The Mandarin said this aloud, his heart warmed.

'And with this lake of water,' said the whisper and the old man, 'we will quench the fire and put it out forever!'

The city turned out in joy to learn that once again they had been saved by the magnificent Emperor of ideas. They ran to the walls and built them nearer to this new vision, singing, not as loudly as before, of course, for they were tired, and not as quickly, for since it had taken a month to rebuild the wall the first time, they had had to neglect business and crops and therefore were somewhat weaker and poorer.

There then followed a succession of horrible and wonderful days, one in another like a nest of frightening boxes.

'Oh, Emperor,' cried the messenger, 'Kwan-Si has rebuilt their walls to resemble a mouth with which to drink all our lake!'

'Then,' said the Emperor, standing very close to his silken screen, 'build our walls like a needle to sew up that mouth!'

'Emperor!' screamed the messenger. 'They make their walls like a sword to break your needle!'

The Emperor held, trembling, to the silken screen. 'Then shift the stones to form a scabbard to sheathe that sword!'

'Mercy,' wept the messenger the following morn, 'they have worked all night and shaped their walls like lightning which will explode and destroy that sheath!'

Sickness spread in the city like a pack of evil dogs. Shops closed. The population, working now steadily for endless months upon the changing of the walls, resembled Death himself, clattering his white bones like musical instruments in the wind. Funerals began to appear in the streets, though it was the middle of summer, a time when all should be tending and harvesting.

The Mandarin fell so ill that he had his bed drawn up by the silken screen and there he lay, miserably giving his architectural orders. The voice behind the screen was weak now, too, and faint, like the wind in the eaves.

'Kwan-Si is an eagle. Then our walls must be a net for that eagle. They are a sun to burn our net. Then we build a moon to eclipse their sun!'

Like a rusted machine, the city ground to a halt.

At last the whisper behind the screen cried out: 'In the name of the gods, send for Kwan-Si!'

Upon the last day of summer the Mandarin of Kwan-Si, very ill and   110
withered away, was carried into our Mandarin's courtroom by four starving footmen. The two mandarins were propped up, facing each other.

Their breaths fluttered like winter winds in their mouths. A voice said:

'Let us put an end to this.'

The old men nodded.

'This cannot go on,' said the faint voice. 'Our people do nothing but rebuild our cities to a different shape every day, every hour. They have no time to hunt, to fish, to love, to be good to their ancestors and their ancestors' children.'

'This I admit,' said the mandarins of the towns of the Cage, the Moon, the   120
Spear, the Fire, the Sword and this, that, and other things.

'Carry us into the sunlight,' said the voice.

The old men were borne out under the sun and up a little hill. In the late summer breeze a few very thin children were flying dragon kites in all the colours of the sun, and frogs and grass, the colour of the sea and the colour of coins and wheat.

The first Mandarin's daughter stood by his bed.

'See,' she said.

'Those are nothing but kites,' said the two old men.

'But what is a kite on the ground?' she said. 'It is nothing. What does it   130
need to sustain it and make it beautiful and truly spiritual?'

'The wind, of course!' said the others.

'And what do the sky and the wind need to make them beautiful?'

'A kite, of course – many kites, to break the monotony, the sameness of the sky. Coloured kites, flying!'

'So,' said the Mandarin's daughter. 'You, Kwan-Si, will make a last rebuilding of your town to resemble nothing more nor less than the wind. And we shall build like a golden kite. The wind will beautify the kite and carry it to wondrous heights. And the kite will break the sameness of the wind's existence and give it purpose and meaning. One without another is   140
nothing. Together, all will be beauty and co-operation and a long and enduring life.'

Whereupon the two mandarins were so overjoyed that they took their first nourishment in days, momentarily were given strength, embraced, and lavished praise upon each other, called the Mandarin's daughter a boy, a man, a stone pillar, a warrior, and a true and unforgettable son. Almost immediately they parted and hurried to their towns, calling out and singing, weakly but happily.

And so, in time, the towns became the Town of the Golden Kite and the Town of the Silver Wind. And harvestings were harvested and business tended again, and the flesh returned and disease ran off like a frightened jackal. And on every night of the year the inhabitants in the Town of the Kite could hear the good clear wind sustaining them. And those in the Town of the Wind could hear the kite singing, whispering, rising, and beautifying them.

'So be it,' said the Mandarin in front of his silken screen.

Ray Bradbury

Questions

1 The reasons for the behaviour of the two towns are contained in the paragraph that begins 'Life was full of symbols...'. Study it carefully and then explain fully in your own words the meaning of its first four sentences.
2 The building and re-building of the walls of the towns followed a pattern of thinking. Explain what that pattern is.
3 What effect did all this building and rebuilding have on the ordinary life of the people of the two towns?
4 How was the government of the town organized **officially**, and who did all the **real** thinking?
5 How and why did the rulers of the two towns eventually come together?
6 Explain in your own words why the Mandarin's daughter chose the kite and the wind as the symbols for the two towns.
7 The story uses a lot of similes (comparisons using 'like' or 'as'). For example: 'Sickness spread in the city like a pack of evil dogs.' (l. 97) Choose two that seem to you to be effective. Write them out. Explain the point of the comparison and say why you think it is effective.
8 This is a story with a 'message'. State what you think that message is and why. How effective is it?

Directed writing

Choose one episode from the story and adapt it as a script for performance on TV or radio. (State which you have chosen.)

Brother Leon

Jerry is a new boy at a Catholic School in the States. Brother Leon is one of the teachers. His appearance suggests that he is a mild man, but he has a reputation for being very strict in class.

Brother Leon was getting ready to put on his show. Jerry knew the symptoms – all the guys knew them. Most of them were freshmen and had been in Leon's class only a month or so but the teacher's pattern had already emerged. First, Leon gave them a reading assignment. Then he'd pace up and down, up and down, restless, sighing, wandering through the aisles, the 5 blackboard pointer poised in his hand, the pointer he used either like a conductor's baton or a musketeer's sword. He'd use the tip to push around a book on a desk or to flick a kid's necktie, scratching gently down some guy's back, poking the pointer as if he were a rubbish collector picking his way through the debris of the classroom. One day, the pointer had rested on 10 Jerry's head for a moment, and then passed on. Unaccountably, Jerry had shivered, as if he'd just escaped some terrible fate.

Now, aware of Leon prowling ceaselessly around the classroom, Jerry kept his eyes on paper although he didn't feel like reading. Two more periods. He looked forward to football practice. 15

'Enough of this crap.'

That was Brother Leon – always trying to shock. Using words like crap and bull and slipping in a few damns and hells once in a while. Actually, he did shock. Maybe because the words were so startling as they issued from this pale and inoffensive-looking little man. Later on, you found out that he 20 wasn't inoffensive, of course. Now, everyone looked up at Leon as that word crap echoed in the room. Ten minutes left – time enough for Leon to perform, to play one of his games. The class looked at him in a kind of horrible fascination. The Brother's glance went slowly around the room, like the ray of a lighthouse sweeping a familiar coast, searching for hidden 25 defects. Jerry felt a sense of dread and anticipation, both at the same time.

'Bailey', Leon said.

'Yes, Brother Leon.' Leon *would* pick Bailey: one of the weak kids, high honour student, but shy, introverted, always reading, his eyes red-rimmed behind the glasses. 30

'Up here,' Leon said, finger beckoning.

Bailey went quietly to the front of the room. Jerry could see a vein throbbing in the boy's temple.

'As you know, gentlemen,' Brother Leon began, addressing the class directly and ignoring Bailey completely although the boy was standing beside 35 him, 'as you know, a certain discipline must be maintained in a school. A line must be drawn between teachers and students. We teachers would love to be one of the boys, of course. But that line of separation must remain. An invisible line, perhaps, but still there.' His moist eyes gleamed. 'After all, you can't see the wind but it's there. You see its handiwork, bending the trees, 40 stirring the leaves . . .'

As he spoke, he gestured, his arm becoming the wind, the pointer in his hand following the direction of the wind and suddenly, without warning, striking Bailey on the cheek. The boy leaped backwards in pain and surprise.

'Bailey, I'm sorry,' Leon said, but his voice lacked apology. Had it been an 45
accident? Or another of Leon's little cruelties?

Now all eyes were on the stricken Bailey. Brother Leon studied him,
looking at him as if he were a specimen under a microscope, as if the
specimen contained the germ of some deadly disease. You had to hand it to
Leon – he was a superb actor. He loved to read short stories aloud taking all 50
the parts, providing all the sound effects. Nobody yawned or fell asleep in
Leon's class. You had to be alert every minute, just as everyone was alert
now, looking at Bailey, wondering what Leon's next move would be. Under
Leon's steady gaze, Bailey had stopped stroking his cheek, even though a
pink welt had appeared, like an evil stain on his flesh. Somehow, the tables 55
were turned. Now it seemed as if Bailey had been at fault all along, that
Bailey had committed an error, had stood in the wrong place at the wrong
time and had caused his own misfortune. Jerry squirmed in his chair. Leon
gave him the creeps, the way he could change the atmosphere in a room
without even speaking a word. 60

'Bailey,' Leon said. But not looking at Bailey, looking at the class as if
they were all in on a joke that Bailey knew nothing about. As if the class and
Leon were banded together in a secret conspiracy.

'Yes, Brother Leon?' Bailey asked, his eyes magnified behind the glasses. A
pause. 65

'Bailey,' Brother Leon said, 'Why do you find it necessary to cheat?' They
say the hydrogen bomb makes no noise: there's only a blinding white flash
that strikes cities dead. The noise comes after the flash, after the silence.
That's the kind of silence that blazed in the classroom now.

Bailey stood speechless, his mouth an open wound. 70

'Is silence an admission of guilt, Bailey?' Brother Leon asked, turning to
the boy at last.

Bailey shook his head frantically. Jerry felt his own head shaking joining
Bailey in silent denial.

'Ah, Bailey,' Leon sighed, his voice fluttering with sadness. 'What are we 75
going to do about you?' Turning towards the class again, buddies with them
– him and the class against the cheat.

'I don't cheat, Brother Leon,' Bailey said, his voice a kind of squeak.

'But look at the evidence, Bailey. Your marks – all A's, no less. Every test,
every paper, every homework assignment. Only a genius is capable of that 80
sort of performance. Do you claim to be a genius, Bailey?' Toying with him.
'I'll admit you look like one – those glasses, that pointed chin, that wild
hair . . .'

Leon leaned towards the class, tossing his own chin, awaiting the approval
of laughter, everything in his manner suggesting the response of laughter 85
from the class. And it came. They laughed. Hey, what's going on here, Jerry
wondered even as he laughed with them. Because Bailey did somehow look
like a genius or at least a caricature of the mad scientist in old movies.

'Bailey,' Brother Leon said, turning his full attention to the boy again as
the laughter subsided. 90

'Yes,' Bailey replied miserably.

'You haven't answered my question.' He walked deliberately to the
window and was suddenly absorbed in the street outside.

Bailey stood alone at the front of the class, as if he were facing a firing squad. Jerry felt his cheeks getting warm, throbbing with warmth. 95

'Well, Bailey?' From Leon at the window, still intent on the world outside.

'I don't cheat, Brother Leon,' Bailey said, a surge of strength in his voice, like he was taking a last stand.

'Then how do you account for all those A's?'

'I don't know.' 100

Brother Leon whirled around. 'Are you perfect, Bailey? All those A's – that implies perfection. Is that the answer, Bailey?'

For the first time, Bailey looked at the class itself, in mute appeal, like something wounded, lost, abandoned.

'Only God is perfect, Bailey.' 105

Jerry's neck began to hurt. And his lungs burned. He realized he'd been holding his breath. He gulped air, carefully, not wanting to move a muscle. He wished he was invisible. He wished he wasn't there in the classroom. He wanted to be out on the football field, fading back.

'Do you compare yourself with God, Bailey?' 110

Cut it out, Brother, cut it out, Jerry cried silently.

'If God is perfect and you are perfect, Bailey, does that suggest something to you?' Bailey didn't answer, eyes wide in disbelief. The class was utterly silent. Jerry could hear the hum of the electric clock.

'The other alternative, Bailey, is that you are not perfect. And, of course, 115 you're not.' Leon's voice softened. 'I know you wouldn't consider anything so sacrilegious.'

'That's right, Brother Leon,' Bailey said, relieved.

'Which leaves us with only one conclusion,' Leon said, his voice bright and triumphant, as if he had made an important discovery. 'You cheat!' 120

In that moment, Jerry hated Brother Leon. He could taste the hate in his stomach – it was acid, foul, burning.

'You're a cheat, Bailey. And a liar.' The words like whips.

You rat, Jerry thought. You bastard.

A voice boomed from the rear of the classroom. 'Aw, let the kid alone!' 125

Leon whipped around. 'Who said that?' His moist eyes glistened.

The bell rang, ending the period. Feet scuffled as the boys pushed back their chairs, preparing to leave, to get out of that terrible place.

'Wait a minute,' Brother Leon said. Softly – but heard by everyone. 'Nobody moves.' 130

The students settled in their chairs again. Brother Leon regarded them pityingly shaking his head, a sad and dismal smile on his lips. 'You poor fools,' he said, 'You idiots. Do you know who's the best one here? The bravest of all?' He placed his hand on Bailey's shoulder. 'Gregory Bailey, that's who. He denied cheating. He stood up to my accusations. He stood his 135 ground! But you, gentlemen, you sat there and enjoyed yourselves. And those of you who didn't enjoy yourselves allowed it to happen, allowed me to proceed. Yes, yes, someone finally protested. 'Aw, let the kid alone.' Mimicking the deep voice perfectly. 'A feeble protest, too little and too late.'

Then he turned to Bailey, touched the top of his head with the pointer as if 140 he were bestowing a knighthood. You did well Bailey. I'm proud of you. You passed the biggest test of all – you were true to yourself.' Bailey's chin was wobbling all over the place. 'Of course you don't cheat, Bailey,' his voice tender and paternal. 'Your classmates out there. They're the cheaters. They cheated you today. They're the ones who doubted you. I never did.' 145

Leon went to his desk. 'Dismissed,' he said, his voice filled with contempt for all of them.

Robert Cormier *The Chocolate War*

Questions

1 What does Brother Leon do while the class are reading, and what effect does it have on them?
2 The narrator knew that Brother Leon tried to shock the class by using bad language. So why was it still shocking?
3 What does the author mean when he says that the class looked at Brother Leon 'in a kind of horrible fascination'? (l. 23–4)
4 Describe the appearance and personality of Bailey.
5 What evidence is given that Brother Leon is 'a superb actor'? (l. 50)
6 Explain fully the comparison used in the three sentences beginning 'They say the hydrogen bomb . . .' and ending '. . . blazed in the classroom now.' (l. 66–69)
7 Why did the class laugh at Bailey?
8 What two arguments did Brother Leon use to prove to Bailey that he must have cheated.
9 As the dialogue between Brother Leon and Bailey proceeds, Jerry's mood gradually changes. Quote the sentences that show this.
10 Why does Brother Leon praise Bailey?
11 Why does he condemn the class?
12 In 100–150 words explain what Brother Leon has set out to do, why he did so and what he thinks he has achieved.
13 Write a character study of Brother Leon based on this extract.
14 Comment on this passage in the light of your experience: is it true to life; could it happen in a British school; do teachers still have this sort of power; are classes as helpless as this?

Directed writing

Write three short accounts of Brother Leon's teaching methods:
a) by a pupil in Jerry's class
b) by the Headmaster
c) by Brother Leon.

Acknowledgements

The publishers would like to thank the following for permission to reproduce photographs and other copywright material:

Anne Bolt, p 117; **Club 18–30**, pp 73, 74 (top); **Commissioner of Police of the Metropolis**, p 85; **Rob Judges**, pp 7, 34, 65; **Kellogg Company**, p 70; **Lloyds Bank**, pp 56, 57; **Mansell Collection**, p 40; **Mary Evans Picture Library**, p 58; **Netherlands Institute for War Documentation**, p 48; **Network/Barry Lewis**, p 114; **Oxfam**, p 81; **Rosie Potter**, p 61; **Saab (UK) Ltd**, pp 50, 51; **Charles Tait**, p 111; **John Topham Picture Library**, p 129; **Which? Magazine**, pp 78, 79.

The photographs on pp 121 and 122 are production stills from *Nuts and Bolts* by **Julia Jones**, produced and directed by Noel Hardy, ILEA TV.

The illustrations are by: Oena Armstrong, Rupert Besley, Judy Brown, Rosamund Fowler, Marie-Hélène Jeeves, Peter Joyce, Liz O'Sullivan, David Parkins, Nick Sharratt, Alistair Taylor, Claire Wright, Melvyn Wright.

The illustration on p 37 is based on material in *The Gaia Atlas of Planet Management*, ed. Norman Myers, Pan Books, 1985, with permission.

The illustrations on p 44 are reproduced by permission of **Calman**.

The diagram on pp 66–67 is reproduced from *The Facts about a Theatre Company* by Peter Lewis, with permission of Andre Deutsch.

The facsimile tourist guide on p 74 is reproduced with the permission of Michelin from their Tourist Guide 'Italy', 10th edition.

The publishers would like to thank the following for permission to reprint copyright material:

Joan Aitken: 'Safe and Sound' from *A Bundle of Nerves* (1976). Reprinted by permission of Victor Gollancz Limited. **Araldite®** is a registered trade mark of Ciba-Geigy Plc. **Pat Barr**: 'I can't even boil an egg' from *The Framing of the Female*. (Kestrel Books 1978). Copyright ©Pat Barr 1978. Reprinted by permission of Penguin Books Limited. **Ray Bradbury**: 'The Golden Kite and the Silver Wind' from *The Stories of Ray Bradbury*. Copyright ©1953 by Ray Bradbury. Reprinted by permission of Harold Matson Company Inc. **Arthur C. Clarke**: from *Profiles of the Future*. Reprinted by permission of Victor Gollancz Limited. **Maureen Cleave**: 'Body Shop' article in *The Observer Colour Supplement* 29.7.84. Reprinted with permission. **Robert Cormier**: 'Brother Leon' from *The Chocolate War*. Reprinted by permission of Victor Gollancz Limited. **Russell Davies**: 'Olympic Darts' in *The Observer Magazine* 19.2.84. Reprinted with permission. **Christopher Dobson and Ronald Payne**: from *The Carlos Complex* (1977). Reprinted by permission of Hodder and Stoughton Limited. **Constance Fitzgibbon**: 'The Blitz Begins' from *London's Burning* (1971). Reprinted by permission of David Higham Associates Limited. **Janet Frame**: 'The Advocate' from *You are Now Entering the Human Heart*. Copyright ©1984 by Janet Frame. Reprinted by kind permission of Curtis Brown Ltd., London on behalf of Janet Frame. **Jane Gardam**: from *The Sidmouth Letters*. Reprinted by permission of Hamish Hamilton Limited. **C. Gausden and N. Crane**: from *Cyclists' Touring Club Route Guide to Cycling in Great Britain and Ireland (1980)*. Reprinted by permission of Oxford Illustrated Press Limited. **Nadine Gordimer**: from *The Soft Voice of the Serpent*, in *Selected Stories* (1953). Reprinted by permission of A. P. Watt Limited. **Graham Greene**: from *A Gun for Sale* (1936). Reprinted by permission of Laurence Pollinger Limited. **Hair and Good Looks Winter 1984**. By permission of IPC Magazines. **The John Harvey Collection**: Harvey Hose, Tring, Herts. HP23 3AJ used by permission. **The Hereford Times**: 'Meal Boycott' and 'Expressing an argument'. Both articles appeared in *The Hereford Times* 15 February 1983. Reprinted with permission. **Clive James**: from *Unreliable Memoirs* (Jonathan Cape Ltd). Reprinted by permission of A. D. Peters & Co. Ltd. **Julia Jones**: 'Nuts and Bolts' from *Studio Scripts Communities* (ed. David Self) 1980. Reprinted by permission of Jill Foster Limited. **Ted Lamb**: from *The Penguin Book of Fishing* (Allen Lane 1979). Copyright © Ted Lamb 1979. Reprinted by permission of Penguin Books Limited. **Fran Lebowitz**: from *Metropolitan Life*. Reprinted by permission of Sidgwick and Jackson Limited. **Laurie Lee**: 'The Village That Lost its Children' from *I Can't Stay Long* (1975). Reprinted by permission of Andre Deutsch Limited. **Prue Leith**: 'Coffee' article that appeared in *The Guardian* February 10 1984. Reprinted by permission of A. D. Peters & Co. Limited. **Peter Lewis**: from *The Facts about a Theatre Company*. Reprinted by permission of Andre Deutsch Limited. **David Lomax**: 'Those Magnificent Women in Their Flying Machines' from *The Listener* 31.5.84. Reprinted by permission of the author. **Penelope Lively**: 'Venice Now and Then' from *Corruption* (1984). Reprinted by permission of William Heinemann Limited. **Douglas Liversidge**: from *The Luddites* (1972). Reprinted by permission of Franklin Watt Limited. **George Mackay Brown**: 'The Box of Fish' from *Andrina and Other Stories* (1983). Reprinted by permission of Chatto and Windus Limited. **Bernard MacLaverty**: 'A Rat and Some Renovations' from *Secrets and Other Stories* (1977). Reprinted by permission of Blackstaff Press Limited. **Norman Mailer**: 'Dead Bird' from *The Naked and the Dead*. Reprinted by permission of Andre Deutsch Limited. **Carla Markham**: 'Occupation' from *The Guardian* May 7 1985. Reprinted by permission of the author. **William Mayne**: from *The Incline*. Reprinted by permission of David Higham Associates Limited. **Norman Myers** (editor): from *The Gaia Atlas of Planet Management* (Pan Books, 1985). Used by permission. **Ogden Nash**: 'The Canary' from *Collected Verse* (1961). Reprinted by permission of Curtis Brown Limited, London. **V. S. Naipaul**: 'The Raffle' from *A Flag on the Island* (1967). Reprinted by permission of Gillon Aitken Limited. **New Society**: 'The Police' in *New Society* 10.5.84. Copyright *New Society*. Reprinted with permission. **Northern Examining Association** for 'Advertising Prunes' from NEA, 1984. Northern Examining Association (Associated Lancashire Schools Examining Board, Joint Matriculation Board, North Regional Examinations Board, North West Regional Examinations Board Yorkshire, and Humberside Regional Examination Board). Reprinted with permission. **Redmond O'Hanlon**: from *Into the Heart of Borneo: An account of a journey made in 1983 to the Mountains of Batu Tiban with James Fenton*. Reprinted by permission of A. D. Peters and Co. Ltd. **Liam O'Flaherty**: 'Trapped' from *The Short Sories of Liam O'Flaherty*. Reprinted by permission of Jonathan Cape Limited. **Karen Payne** (ed): 'Writing Home' from *Between Ourselves*. (Michael Joseph Limited.) **J. M. Peyton**: from *A Midsummer Night's Death* (1978). Reprinted by permission of Oxford University Press. **Lynne Reid Banks**: 'Something To Say' from *One More River*. Reprinted by permission of Vallentine Mitchell and Co. Ltd. **Frank Sargeson**: 'Boy' from *Collected Stories* (Blackwood & Janet Paul 1964). Reprinted by permission of The Bodley Head. **Rukshana Smith**: from *Sumitra's Story* (1982). Reprinted by permission of The Bodley Head. **Alan Spence**: 'Christian Endeavour' from *Panther Book of Scottish Short Stories*, (ed. James Campbell, 1984). Reprinted by permission of William Collins and Co. Limited. **Wilfred Thesiger**: from *The Marsh Arabs*. Reprinted by kind permission of Curtis Brown Limited, London. **Jon Vogler**: 'Re-cycling Waste in the Third World' from *The Listener* 12.7.84. Reprinted by permission of the author. **Robert Waterhouse**: article about Vandalism, *The Guardian* March 21 1979. **Tony Wilkinson**: 'Marathon Mentality – the risks sportsmen run', from *The Listener* 31 May 1984. Reprinted by permission of the author.

Every effort has been made to trace and contact copyright holders but this has not always been possible. We apologise for any infringement of copyright.

Cover illustration: *Le Marinier* by Fernand Léger, 1918.
The Bridgman Art Library/© DACS 1986.